BBC

Bitesize
AQA GCSE (9-1)
GEOGRAPHY
REVISION GUIDE

T0346006

Series Consultant:
Harry Smith

Author:
Michael Chiles

Contents

✓ Tick off each topic as you go.

How to use this book

Use the features in this book to focus your revision, track your progress through the topics and practise your exam skills.

② Features to help you revise

Scan the **QR codes** to visit the BBC Bitesize website. It will link straight through to more revision resources on that subject.

Each bite-sized chunk has a **timer** to indicate how long it will take. Use them to plan your revision sessions.

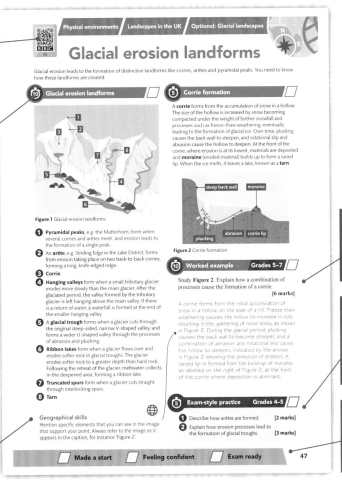

Topics that are related to **geographical skills** are explained in callouts and in the Geographical skills section at the back.

Complete **worked examples** demonstrate how to approach exam-style questions.

Test yourself with exam-style practice at the end of each page and check your answers at the back of the book.

Tick boxes allow you to track the sections you've revised. Revisit each page to embed your knowledge.

② Exam focus features

The *About your exam* section at the start of the book gives you all the key information about your exams, as well as showing you how to identify the different questions.

Throughout the topic pages you will also find green *Exam skills* pages. These work through an extended exam-style question and provide further opportunities to practise your skills.

② ActiveBook and app

This Revision Guide comes with a **free online edition**. Follow the instructions from inside the front cover to access your ActiveBook.

You can also download the **free BBC Bitesize app** to access revision flash cards and quizzes.

If you do not have a QR code scanner, you can access all the links in this book from your ActiveBook or visit **www.pearsonschools.co.uk/BBCBitesizeLinks**.

Your Geography GCSE

This page will tell you everything you need to know about the structure of your upcoming AQA GCSE Geography exam.

 About the exam papers

You will have to take **three papers** as part of your AQA GCSE Geography qualification. The papers will test your knowledge, understanding and geographical skills. Each of the papers has a different focus. Paper 1 is all about physical environments and Paper 2 is all about human environments. Paper 3 focuses on the application of your geographical skills as well as your knowledge of both physical and human environments. There are some optional topics in Paper 1 and Paper 2.

Paper 1
Living with the physical environment
1 hour 30 minutes
88 marks in total

Paper 2
Challenges in the human environment
1 hour 30 minutes
88 marks in total

Paper 3
Geographical applications
1 hour 15 minutes
76 marks in total

 Papers 1 and 2

Papers 1 and 2 have three sections, A, B and C.

For Paper 1, Section B, you only need to have studied **either** hot deserts or cold environments.

In Paper 1 Section C, you will have the choice to answer **two** of three questions about:

- Coastal landscapes in the UK
- River landscapes in the UK
- Glacial landscapes in the UK.

In Paper 2, Section C, you will only need to answer **one** question about:

- Food
- Water
- Energy.

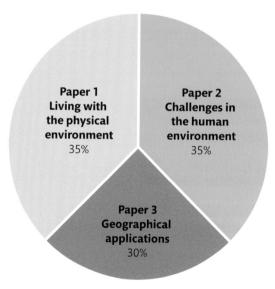

 Paper 3: Geographical applications

The third paper is different from Paper 1 and Paper 2. Ahead of the exam, you will be given a resource booklet and you will undertake two geographical investigations. You need to apply your knowledge of these in the written assessment.

Section A: Issue evaluation

12 weeks before the exam, you will receive a booklet containing different resources, such as maps, photos, graphs and texts. The resources will all relate to a particular issue linked to one of the compulsory topics you have studied.

Before the exam, you should familiarise yourself with the resources and make notes in your booklet. You will be given a clean copy of the booklet in the exam.

Section B: Fieldwork

Fieldwork is an essential part of your Geography qualification. In the exam, you will be assessed on both of the geographical investigations you have undertaken. You will also be expected to apply what you know to new enquiries.

Made a start | Feeling confident | Exam ready

Multiple choice

Multiple-choice questions give you several options to choose from. You must indicate the correct answer by marking your choice clearly.

Multiple-choice questions usually start with the command word 'identify'.

1 Identify which statement correctly describes the process of plucking.
Shade **one** circle only.

[1 mark]

A the action of the glacier rubbing rocks, like sandpaper, against the bedrock

B the action of the glacier removing loose fragments as it moves

C the action of water freezing in the rock, expanding and exerting pressure, leading to cracks

D the action of the glacier eroding the sides of a valley as it moves

Clearly shade in the circle that you think is the correct answer.

If you are unsure of the answer, use what you know to rule out the incorrect options.

Some questions require you to engage with a map or graph. Look at the figure carefully and make sure you understand what it is showing before you answer the question.

2

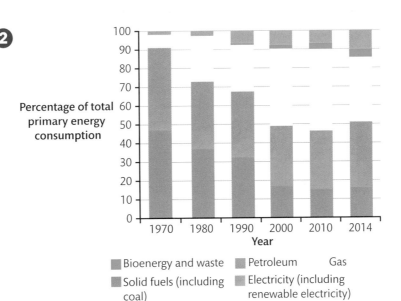

Figure 1 Total primary energy consumption by fuel, UK (1970–2014)

Using **Figure 1**, which two of the following statements are true?
Shade **two** circles only.

A The UK's reliance on gas is increasing.

B The UK's reliance on solid fuels has decreased since 1970.

C In 1990, 50% of the UK's primary energy consumption was petroleum.

D In 2014, 10% of the UK's primary energy consumption was electricity.

If you want to change your answer, cross out the incorrect circle and shade the correct one.

 Made a start   **Feeling confident**   **Exam ready**

Short answers

Short-answer questions come in a variety of forms and are the most common type of questions. They are worth 1–2 marks.

② Command words

- ☑ calculate – work out the value
- ☑ complete – finish the task by adding information
- ☑ give – produce an answer from memory
- ☑ identify – name or characterise
- ☑ state – express in clear terms
- ☑ outline – set out the main characteristics
- ☑ describe – set out characteristics
- ☑ explain – set out purposes or reasons

② Exam focus

Short-answer questions should be quick to complete, so you should aim to spend only 1 or 2 minutes on each one.

⑩ Exam explainer

Make sure you read the question carefully so you know how many points to include in your answer – this question asks for two factors.

1 Give **one** reason why tropical storms lose their energy.

[1 mark]

This type of one mark question only needs a short answer.

2 State **two** factors that affect water availability.

[2 marks]

3

Figure 1 Philodendron plants grow in tropical rainforests

Using **Figure 1**, describe one plant adaptation in tropical rainforests.

[2 marks]

Many short answer questions use images. Check that you are using the correct figure and look at it carefully.

Some **describe** questions are worth 4 or 6 marks and require more detail. Look at the number of marks available for a question to tell you how much detail you need to provide in your answer – the more marks available, the more detailed your answer should be.

 Made a start   **Feeling confident**   ☑ **Exam ready**

Levelled response

Some questions assess the quality and level of your response. You need to communicate clearly and provide the right amount of detail.

 Exam explainer

4 mark questions have two levels:
1. basic
2. clear.
A clear answer interprets, evaluates or analyses geographical information or resources. It can sometimes involve making a judgement about a particular issue based on balanced information.

1 Look at the map in **Figure 1**.

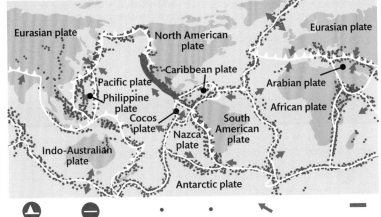

destructive boundary   constructive boundary   earthquakes   volcanoes   direction of plate movement   conservative boundary

Figure 1 The distribution of earthquakes and volcanoes

Using **Figure 1**, compare the global distribution of earthquakes and volcanoes.

[4 marks]

You could be asked to study a resource, such as a map, graph, photo, table or sketch drawing, in any of your exams. For this type of question, it is important you look at the resource provided carefully so you understand exactly what it is showing before you begin to write your answer.

2 Describe and explain the formation of a waterfall.

[6 marks]

Include specific details from the map in your answer, such as names of tectonic plates.

6–9 mark questions have three levels:
1. basic
2. clear
3. detailed.
A detailed answer shows understanding of geographical topics and knowledge of specific information. It is presented in a clear and unbiased way.

If asked to **describe** and explain, refer to specific features and develop your points. Use specialist terminology accurately to show your knowledge.

 Command words

- ✓ describe – set out characteristics
- ✓ suggest – present a possible case
- ✓ explain – set out purposes or reasons
- ✓ compare – identify similarities and differences

 Structure your answers

- ✓ Make a **point** – for example: *Deforestation can lead to the loss of biodiversity in rainforests.*
- ✓ **Develop** your point – for example: *This is because it destroys the natural habitat of many plant and animal species so they can no longer live there.*
- ✓ **Link** your point back to the question – for example: *This reduces biodiversity because there will be a loss of plant and animal species.*

Extended answers

Some questions require you to write a longer answer that demonstrates your knowledge and understanding of Geography and your ability to develop ideas in a structured way.

 Command words

- ✓ assess – make an informed judgement
- ✓ discuss – present key points about different ideas
- ✓ to what extent – judge the importance or success of a strategy
- ✓ justify – support an opinion or case with evidence
- ✓ evaluate – make a judgement using evidence

 Exam focus

Some extended prose questions assess your accuracy of spelling, punctuation, grammar (SPaG) and specialist terminology. These will always be indicated by the number of marks available.

Aim to spend 10–12 minutes answering these questions, including time for checking your work.

 Exam explainer

In an **assess** question, demonstrate that you have considered the facts involved and make an informed decision.

1 For a named example of one area of UK coastline, assess how successful a coastal management scheme has been in protecting the coast.

[9 marks]
[+ 3 SPaG marks]

In this question there are extra marks available for spelling, punctuation, grammar and specialist terminology.

2 For a cold environment that you have studied, to what extent does it provide both opportunities and challenges for development?

[9 marks]

Include detailed information about one of the case studies you have learned about. You need to judge both sides of the issue – in this case challenges and opportunities.

For **discuss** questions, present the key points about the issue and include specific details. You do not need to come to a conclusion about an issue.

3 Discuss the effects of urbanisation upon people in a city in a lower income country you have studied.

[9 marks]

4 Evaluate the impacts of deforestation upon a tropical rainforest you have studied.

[9 marks]

This **evaluate** question requires you to use and display your knowledge of both physical and human geographical issues. Back up your statements with evidence.

Defining natural hazards

A natural hazard is an extreme event with the potential to cause major damage to humans, properties and the environment.

(5) Types of natural hazards

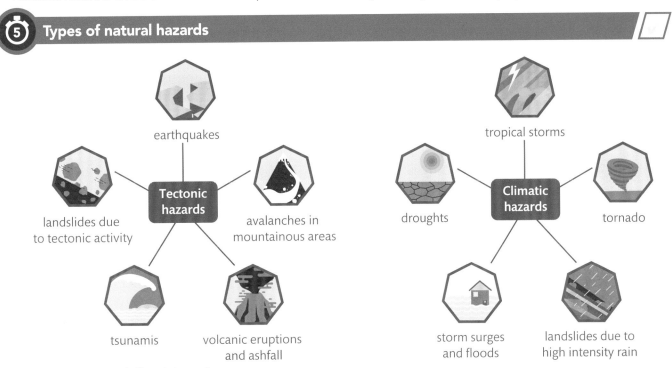

Figure 1 Tectonic and climatic hazards

(5) Three factors affecting hazard risk

Climate change
Rising global temperatures are increasing the frequency and intensity of tropical storms, storm surges, floods, landslides and droughts, and leading to a higher **natural hazard** risk in more areas of the world. This is increasing the number of people who may be affected by natural hazards.

Location
The proportion of the world's population living in cities in seismically active areas is growing. A well-known example is the San Andreas Fault, a plate boundary where earthquakes and tsunamis can occur. It extends through California, a state in which 95 per cent of the population lives in urban areas.

Urbanisation
A growing proportion of the world's population live in urban areas. Increasing numbers of people live on flood plains or areas at risk of landslides or flooding by the sea, often with no choice. As the global population continues to expand, the number of properties and people living in densely populated areas at risk of flood hazards will increase.

(5) Worked example　　Grades 1–3

Give **two** factors that could increase vulnerability to the effects of a tsunami in a coastal area. **[2 marks]**

You only need to state the factors for this question, not explain them.

Humans in coastal areas are more vulnerable to the effects of a tsunami if the area is low-lying and densely populated.

Exam focus
For this question, you will need to clearly explain how your chosen factors can lead to an increased risk.

(5) Exam-style practice　　Grades 5–6

Explain the factors affecting the level of risk of a natural hazard.

[4 marks]

Distribution of earthquakes and volcanoes

Scientists use historical data to map the previous occurrence of earthquakes and volcanic activity, which enables geographers to identify patterns in their distribution.

(5) Plate tectonics theory

The crust is the outer layer of the Earth. There are two types of crust:

1 **continental crust** (thick and formed from older rocks)

2 **oceanic crust** (thin and formed from younger rocks).

Oceanic crust is denser than continental crust. The Earth's crust is divided into plates. Scientists believe that these plates move due to convection currents occurring deep in the mantle. This movement generates vast amounts of energy at plate margins, which results in earthquakes and volcanic eruptions.

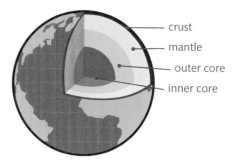

Figure 1 The Earth consists of four layers

crust
mantle
outer core
inner core

(10) Global distribution of earthquakes and volcanoes

Earthquakes usually occur at destructive and conservative plate margins. Minor earthquakes can occur at constructive plate margins. **Intraplate earthquakes** occur away from plate margins. The reasons for this are not fully understood, but it is thought that they are caused by convection currents in the Earth's mantle.

You can revise the types of plate margin on page 3.

Volcanoes usually occur at constructive plate margins but can also occur at destructive plate margins. Earthquakes can be triggered by human activities, such as underground mining. The ring of volcanoes (and earthquakes) around the Pacific plate is known as the 'Ring of Fire'.

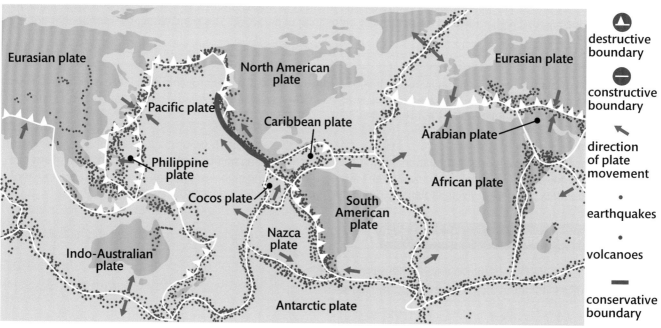

Figure 2 The distribution of volcanoes and earthquakes in relation to plate margins

Geographical skills
Use **PQE** to describe a distribution on a map.
P – Give the general **pattern**.
Q – **Quantify** (support) the pattern.
E – Identify any **exceptions** (anomalies).

(5) Exam-style practice   Grade 4

Look at **Figure 2**. Describe the distribution of volcanoes.

[3 marks]

Plate margin activity

You need to know which hazards occur at plate margins, and why and how they occur there.

⑮ Plate margins

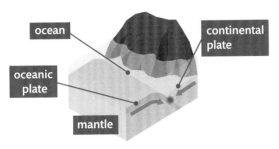

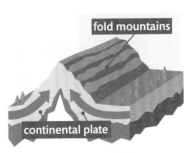

Destructive plate margin

- A continental plate and an oceanic plate move towards each other. The denser oceanic plate is forced under the continental plate, where it melts and forms magma. Under immense pressure, the magma is released in violent volcanic eruptions.
- A build-up of friction between the plates leads to a sudden release of pressure, causing powerful earthquakes.
- The Andes formed when the denser Nazca plate was forced under the continental South American plate.

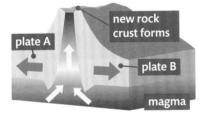

Constructive plate margin

- Two plates move away from each other.
- Volcanoes form as magma rises to the surface. The magma cools and solidifies to form new land and volcanic islands.
- Earthquakes sometimes occur on constructive plate boundaries.
- Earthquakes and volcanoes are usually less violent at constructive plate margins.
- The North American and Eurasian plates are moving away from each other at the Mid-Atlantic ridge.

Destructive plate margin: collision zones

- Two continental plates move towards each other. The land between the plates is pushed upwards, creating **fold mountains**.
- Earthquakes occur at destructive collision plate margins, but volcanoes do not.
- The collision between the Indian plate and the Eurasian plate formed the Himalayas.

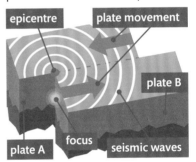

Conservative plate margin

- Two plates slide past each other in opposite directions, or in the same direction but at different speeds.
- A build-up of friction between the two plates can lead to the sudden release of pressure, causing earthquakes, but not volcanoes.
- At the San Andreas Fault in California, the Pacific plate is sliding faster than the North American plate, which is moving in the same direction. This has caused severe earthquakes around San Francisco.

⑤ Worked example   Grade 5

Explain how earthquakes are formed at destructive plate margins.   **[4 marks]**

Two tectonic plates move towards each other because of convection currents. Where the two plates meet, the denser (oceanic) plate is forced beneath the oceanic or continental plate. The plates slide against each other and cause a build-up of intense pressure. The sudden release of this energy causes an earthquake.

Clearly explain the physical processes that cause these hazards. You can give a specific example of a plate margin to support your answer.

⑤ Exam-style practice   Grade 5

Describe how volcanoes form at constructive plate margins.   **[2 marks]**

Earthquake effects

You may be asked to compare the effects of a tectonic hazard between two areas of contrasting wealth. This page compares the earthquakes in Nepal and Ecuador.

 Named example

Nepal and Ecuador

	Nepal (2015)	**Ecuador (2016)**
Primary effects	• Over 8000 people were killed and many thousands more were injured. • Roads and more than 600,000 buildings in Kathmandu and nearby towns were either damaged or destroyed. • The cost of the damage was estimated to be between \$5 billion and \$10 billion.	• 650 people were killed and approximately 12,500 people were injured. • Roads and more than 7000 buildings were damaged or destroyed. • The cost of the widespread damage to buildings and infrastructure was estimated to be approximately \$3 billion.
Secondary effects	• Approximately 2.8 million people were left homeless by the earthquake. • Landslides destroyed nearby rural villages. • The earthquake also triggered an avalanche on Mount Everest, killing 19 people and causing hundreds to be left stranded at camps above the avalanche.	• Over 26,000 people were left homeless by the earthquake. • The tremors were felt in the nearby countries of Peru and Colombia. • Many people were left without power and phone lines.

 Comparing the effects of earthquakes

Despite being the same magnitude – 7.8 on the Richter scale – the effects of the earthquakes in Nepal, a low income country (LIC), and Ecuador, a newly emerging economy (NEE), differed considerably. The effects of tectonic hazards tend to be much more severe in LICs than in NEEs or high income countries (HICs).

Primary effects are the immediate results of a tectonic hazard, whereas secondary effects are the aftermath of the tectonic hazard, and are often the result of the primary effects. For example, a primary effect of the Nepal earthquake was that more than 600,000 buildings were destroyed; a secondary effect was approximately 2.8 million people being left homeless.

The effects of the earthquake were much worse in Nepal than in Ecuador – over ten times as many people were killed in Nepal. LICs, such as Nepal, cannot afford expensive seismic monitoring systems, so cannot predict tectonic hazards and evacuate people. In addition, buildings in LICs tend to have inferior construction compared with those in HICs, which could cause them to collapse. This could cause death or homelessness.

 Worked example **Grade 5**

Using **two** named examples you have studied, explain the possible primary effects of earthquakes.

[4 marks]

One of the possible primary effects of earthquakes is deaths and injuries; for example, the Nepal earthquake in 2015 killed over 8000 people and the Ecuador earthquake in 2016 killed 650 people. Another primary effect is the damage to infrastructure such as roads, which makes transport difficult.

Exam focus

Remember, an **assess** question is asking you to make a judgement – use your knowledge about the effects of earthquakes from the named example you have studied to come to an informed conclusion in your answer.

  Exam-style practice **Grades 5–9**

Assess the extent to which the effects of earthquakes are more severe in an LIC.

[9 marks] [+3 SPaG marks]

 Made a start **Feeling confident** **Exam ready**

Earthquake responses

You may be asked to compare the responses to a tectonic hazard between two areas of contrasting wealth. This page compares the earthquakes in Nepal and Ecuador.

 Named example

Nepal and Ecuador

	Nepal (2015)	Ecuador (2016)
Immediate response	• The government of Nepal initiated a state of emergency, with the army deployed to assist with the search and rescue efforts. • The coordination of international aid was established by the United Nations (UN) through the creation of the Nepal Earthquake Flash Appeal. Many countries and individuals contributed, and over £87 million was raised. • Neighbouring countries like India, China and Pakistan provided aid and assisted in the rescue operations.	• 10,000 soldiers and 4600 police officers were deployed to assist victims. • Emergency medical services were provided to people in the worst affected areas by organisations such as the International Medical Corps. • Temporary shelters and mobile hospitals were built in Pedernales and Portoviejo. • K9 units with specially trained dogs were brought in by the police to assist with the rescue operations.
Long-term response	• GeoHazards International set up the Kathmandu Valley Earthquake Risk Management Project to raise awareness of earthquake risk and prepare an action plan for managing the risk. • Nepal and the UN worked together to establish a national building code to improve the structure of buildings.	• Non-governmental organisations (NGOs) like Oxfam worked with local communities to raise awareness of good hygiene practices to limit the spread of waterborne diseases. • Oxfam worked to rebuild water supply systems in the municipality of San Vicente.

 Comparing the responses

Immediate responses

In Nepal, healthcare provision and medicine was not as widely available, and people were largely reliant on international aid for medical attention.

In Ecuador, there was a widespread and organised emergency response by the government, deploying soldiers, police officers and specially trained dogs, whereas in Nepal, an LIC, the emergency response was helped considerably by other countries.

Long-term responses

In Nepal, long-term responses were unplanned and therefore comparatively basic, such as raising the awareness of earthquake risk.

In Ecuador, a wealthier country, emergency hospitals were provided soon after the earthquake. Long-term responses were well organised and focused upon preventing secondary effects, such as the spread of diseases.

Exam focus

To achieve maximum marks in this question, you need to accurately use specific information about a named example you have studied to support the points you make.

 Worked example Grade 4

Describe **one** immediate response and **one** long-term response to a tectonic hazard. [4 marks]

An immediate response to a tectonic hazard such as an earthquake is the deployment of emergency services for search and rescue operations, for example the use of the army after the 2015 Nepal earthquake. The work of non-governmental organisations (NGOs) like Oxfam is an example of a long-term response, helping to rebuild water supplies, like those affected during the 2016 Ecuador earthquake.

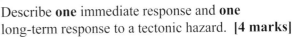

For this question you need to name **one** immediate and **one** long-term response, and describe each. Do not name more than one of each type, as you will not get extra marks.

 Exam-style practice Grade 5

Explain how NGOs assist in the response to tectonic hazards. [4 marks]

 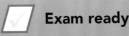

Living with natural hazards

Some people have no choice but to live with the uncertainty of natural hazards, while others actively choose to live in these dangerous areas.

 Opportunities in hazardous areas

Evacuation
Monitoring by scientists means that people can be warned of, and evacuated away from, some hazards.

Infrequency
The infrequency of volcanic hazards mean that some people think they will not be affected in their lifetime.

Tourism
Volcanoes and their surrounding landscapes are tourist attractions, providing jobs for local people as tour guides and boosting the local economy. For example, in Hawaii there are multiple tours available around active volcanoes, some of which cost hundreds of dollars per person.

Building design
In developed countries like the USA, improved building design has decreased the potential damage from an earthquake.

Choosing to live in hazardous areas

Geothermal
Volcanic activity can provide opportunities for generating geothermal energy. In Iceland, approximately 66 per cent of all energy comes from geothermal energy.

Fertile soils
Volcanoes can bring benefits that outweigh the risks for some people. For example, minerals in volcanic ash, such as nitrogen and potassium, can create rich fertile soils for farmers, increasing crop yields.

Figure 1 Geothermal energy pipeline in Iceland

Figure 2 Farmers ploughing their fields near Mount Agung, a volcano in Bali

 Worked example   Grade 5

Explain the reasons why people choose to live in areas with volcanic hazards.

[4 marks]

One of the reasons people choose to live near volcanoes is because they are usually good places to farm crops. Volcanic ash provides a nutrient-rich soil, which increases crop yields. This increases the potential income of local farmers. Also, many volcanic areas have spectacular surrounding landscapes that attract tourists. This benefits locals as it creates employment opportunities, for example as guides for tourists.

For this question, you are not expected to discuss a named example, but any that you did include would support the points you make.

 Exam-style practice   Grades 3–4

Explain **one** economic reason why people choose to live in volcanically active areas.   [2 marks]

Reducing the risk

Volcanoes and earthquakes are natural hazards that can be unpredictable, but there are a number of strategies that are used to reduce the risks.

 15 Risk reduction strategies

Monitoring
- **Thermal imaging equipment** is used to detect the amount of heat coming from a volcano, which can help scientists to predict if an eruption is likely.
- **Chemical sensors** are used to assess gas levels in a volcano, which can help scientists to detect sulfur levels. Changes to sulfur levels may indicate changes in the magma supply, and therefore indicate a possible eruption.
- **Seismometers** can be used to record earthquake activity in and around volcanoes.
- **GPS, tiltmeters and laser beams** can measure ground deformation to monitor changes in the shape of a volcano and detect movements in the Earth's plates.

Protection
- **Exclusion zones** – areas where people are not allowed to live, and where access is limited depending on volcanic activity – can be set up based on previous eruptions to protect people, as on the island of Montserrat following the eruption in 1997.
- **Earth embankments** can be built around a volcano to try to divert the flow of magma.
- **Earthquake-proof buildings** can be constructed to reduce the potential impact from the tremors. They may use features like shock absorbers, a reinforced steel structure and counterweights.
- **Earthquake drills** can be practised to ensure people are prepared for the event.

Prediction
Volcanic eruptions can be predicted by scientists who carefully monitor a volcano's activity. Predicting earthquakes is much more difficult due to an absence of warning signs. However, most earthquakes do occur in predictable locations. Previous plate activity is evaluated when considering risk.

Planning
Hazard maps indicate which areas are most at risk of tectonic hazards. They are produced by studying volcanic deposits. The use of hazard maps enables decision makers to decide on the locations of key infrastructure.

Planning and practising evacuation enables people to escape more quickly and safely.

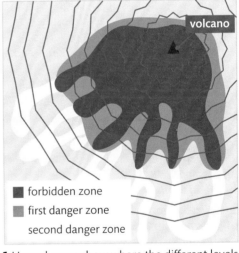

Figure 1 Hazard maps show where the different levels of risk are for specific types of hazard, such as lava flows.

 2 Worked example | Grades 1–2

Which **one** of the following statements describes a strategy used to monitor volcanoes?
Shade **one** circle only.

[1 mark]

A building earth embankments ○

B practising earthquake drills ○

C using thermal imaging equipment ◉

Options A and B describe a protection strategy. Option C is correct because it describes a monitoring strategy.

5 Exam-style practice | Grade 5

Explain how protection and planning can reduce the effects of earthquakes.

[4 marks]

General atmospheric circulation model

The Earth's atmosphere is constantly moving, transferring heat energy from one location to another via atmospheric circulation cells. These cells have distinctive characteristics that cause multiple weather systems.

Circulation cells

Solar radiation is spread over a wider area of distribution at the poles than at the equator. In both hemispheres, the redistribution of heat energy is caused by three atmospheric circulation cells: the Polar cell, the Ferrel cell and the Hadley cell. Heat energy is transferred where the cells meet.

1 Warmed air rises at the equator, causing low pressure. The air moves north and south and cools to create **Hadley cells**. At latitudes of 30° north and south, the cooled air sinks, causing high pressure.

2 Cooled air that moves back towards the equator is known as **trade winds**, while the rest of the air moves towards the poles, forming part of the **Ferrel cells**.

3 At latitudes of 60° north and south, the warmer air of the Ferrel cells meets colder polar air at the polar fronts. A polar jet stream is formed above this which drives the unstable atmosphere. The warmer air rises to form **Polar cells**. This air travels north to the poles, where it cools and sinks, forming areas of high pressure.

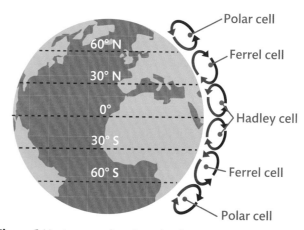

Figure 1 Heat energy flow in a circulation cell

How circulation cells affect weather

Air blows from areas of high pressure to areas of low pressure. The winds are affected by the **Coriolis effect**, which deflects the winds to the right in the northern hemisphere and to the left in the southern hemisphere.

The different circulation cells and variations in **pressure belts** and **surface winds** cause different weather conditions depending on location.

- The Polar easterlies create dry, cold weather conditions near the poles.
- The trade winds gather moisture as they blow from east to west, which can result in rainfall when they blow over land in tropical regions such as Hawaii.

> The Coriolis effect is due to the spin of the Earth acting on the movement of the air flow.

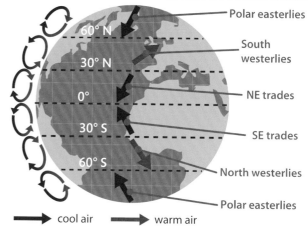

Figure 2 Global atmospheric circulation

Worked example — Grade 3

State the **two** circulation cells that meet at latitudes of 60° north and south.

[2 marks]

The Ferrel cell and the Polar cell

Exam-style practice — Grade 5

Explain how global atmospheric circulation contributes towards distinctive weather and climate patterns.

[4 marks]

 Made a start 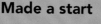 **Feeling confident** 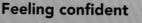 **Exam ready**

Distribution of tropical storms

Tropical storms are known as **cyclones**, **hurricanes** or **typhoons**, depending on where they develop in the world. You need to know how, where and when they occur.

 Global distribution of tropical storms

Tropical storms form in the tropics between approximately 5° and 30° latitude (between the Tropic of Cancer and the Tropic of Capricorn, but not normally at the equator). They are confined to the tropics because they require certain conditions to form. They tend to occur in the northern tropics between June and November, and in the southern tropics between November and April. Tropical storms are given different names depending on where they occur in the world:

- **hurricanes** begin in the *Atlantic Ocean*
- **typhoons** begin in the north-west *Pacific Ocean*
- **cyclones** begin in the *South Pacific* or the *Indian Ocean*.

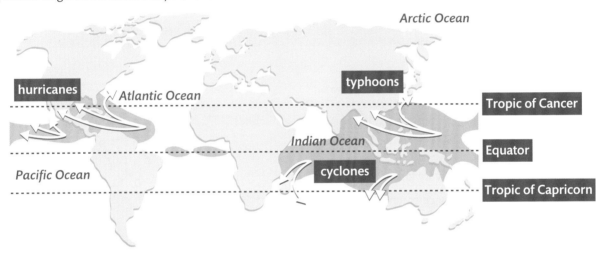

Figure 1 Global distribution and movement of tropical storms – the arrows show that they tend to move westwards, because they are affected by the prevailing trade winds.

 Conditions needed

- ✓ Warm sea temperatures – at least 26.5 °C at the sea's surface
- ✓ A lot of water vapour in the atmosphere
- ✓ Low pressure disturbances and smaller storms that can join to form a tropical storm
- ✓ Rapidly cooling water vapour, which forms cumulonimbus clouds
- ✓ Warm air rising from the ocean, which is pulled into a column of clouds
- ✓ Coriolis effect creating spin (the force isn't usually strong enough to create a tropical storm within 5° of the equator)

Exam focus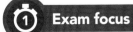

Before your exam, make sure you know the location of the seven continents and the five major oceans.

 **Worked example** **Grades 1–2**

Using **Figure 1**, which **one** of the following statements is correct? Shade **one** circle only.
[1 mark]

A Hurricanes can form in the *Atlantic Ocean* and travel west towards Mexico and the USA.

B Cyclones can form in the *Pacific Ocean* and travel east towards Indonesia. ◯

C Cyclones can form in the *Indian Ocean* and travel north towards Africa.

Exam-style practice **Grades 1–2**

State **one** factor that influences the distribution of tropical storms.
[1 mark]

Causes and features of tropical storms

The term **tropical storm** refers to the low pressure systems that form over tropical or subtropical waters.

⑤ Key features of tropical storms

- ☑ Tropical storms create very low pressure, high winds, and heavy rainfall.
- ☑ They form a cylinder of rising, spiralling air (Coriolis effect) surrounding an **eye** of descending cool air.
- ☑ The eye of the storm is a region of clear skies where cool air is descending.
- ☑ Cloud banks known as the **eye wall** surround the eye. The strongest winds tend to occur in the eye wall.
- ☑ Tropical storms can be hundreds of kilometres in width. The largest ever recorded, Typhoon Tip (1979), was over 1000 km wide.

⑩ Formation of a tropical storm

1 Hurricanes require a source of warm, moist air and warm ocean temperatures (at least 26.5 °C at the sea's surface). This restricts where they can form.

2 The warm ocean causes water to evaporate, forming cumulonimbus clouds, and warm air rising rapidly from the ocean causes thunderstorms.

3 These converge, and an area of very low pressure forms.

4 As the air rises it starts to spin, accelerating in speed.

5 The faster the wind speed, the lower the pressure at the centre, and the stronger the hurricane.

6 The rising air cools and condenses, and more cumulonimbus clouds form and grow, bringing rain, thunder and lightning.

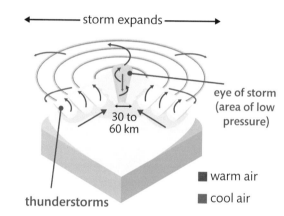

Figure 1 A tropical storm

⑤ Climate change impacts

Rising sea temperatures could influence the **distribution** of tropical storms, with more storms occurring outside the current distribution.

Some scientists believe that there is a link between rising sea temperatures and an increase in the **frequency** and **intensity** of tropical storms.

If global warming continues at its current rate, possible effects include increased storm intensity and higher wind speeds in tropical storms, which could make them more destructive than any historic tropical storm.

② Worked example Grades 2–3

Give **two** characteristics of a tropical storm.

[2 marks]

One characteristic of a tropical storm is that it has very low pressure. A second characteristic is that it has an eye wall that surrounds the eye.

You could write about other characteristics of tropical storms, such as the different parts of the storm and their features, and the conditions they need in order to form.

⑤ Exam-style practice Grade 5

Explain how tropical storms are formed. [4 marks]

 Made a start　 **Feeling confident**　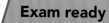 **Exam ready**

Typhoon Haiyan

You may be asked to give details about a tropical storm that you have studied. This page analyses the primary and secondary effects of Typhoon Haiyan.

 Named example

Typhoon Haiyan

Date: 2 November 2013

Origin: western *Pacific Ocean*, close to the Federated States of Micronesia

Direction: it moved west over the Philippines

Maximum wind speeds: about 313 km/h (a Category 5 hurricane)

Physical impacts: It caused a storm surge, where strong winds and low pressure caused the sea level to rise by over 7 metres high in some areas, including the storm surge that hit the town of Tacloban.

Human impacts: More than 14 million people in at least 46 provinces were affected.

Figure 1 Much of the damage was sustained on the islands of Samar and Leyte.

 Primary and secondary effects

Primary effects	Secondary effects
widespread flooding	landslides and blocked roads
• 6300 deaths • 1061 people recorded missing	• low morale • strain on medical resources • homelessness • loss of jobs and income
approximately 1.4 million properties (including homes and businesses) destroyed or damaged	
very large quantities of trees and topsoil uprooted	large amounts of carbon dioxide released
• rice crops and coconut plantations destroyed	• food security issues • damage to the economy
damage to infrastructure	lack of clean water and sanitation leading to disease

 Worked example **Grade 5**

Explain **one** primary and **one** secondary effect a tropical storm has on people. **[4 marks]**

One primary effect a tropical storm has on people is loss of life and serious injuries, as seen during Typhoon Haiyan, which killed 6300 people. A secondary effect a tropical storm has on people is homelessness due to the considerable devastation to buildings. Typhoon Haiyan damaged or destroyed approximately 1.4 million buildings, leaving millions of people homeless.

Primary effects are the initial direct impacts of a tropical storm on people and property, such as damage to buildings and loss of life.

Secondary effects are the indirect impacts, which are often long-term, such as homelessness and damage to the economy. Make sure you know examples of primary effects and secondary effects for your named example.

 Responses to Typhoon Haiyan

Immediate responses
- Foreign governments, such as the UK and Canada, sent shelter kits; USA and Japan sent water and household items.
- Evacuation centres provided temporary shelter for the homeless.

Long-term responses
- Many homes were rebuilt away from areas of flood risk.
- Livelihood support programmes provided cash grants for debris clearance and recycling, and assisted coconut farmers with recovering their damaged trees.
- Philippine Red Cross volunteers helped survivors to rebuild their homes, and educated people on planning for the future.

 Exam-style practice **Grades 5–8**

Using an example you have studied, describe immediate and long-term responses to a tropical storm. **[6 marks]**

 Made a start Feeling confident 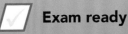 Exam ready

Planning for tropical storms

Tropical storms can have significant effects on people and the environment, so it is important to use strategies such as monitoring, prediction, protection and planning to reduce the effects.

(10) Reducing the hazard risk

Monitoring and prediction

Scientists use **satellite** and **radar** technology with weather charts and complex computer software to track the development and approach of a tropical storm.

The USA, a HIC, has a structured and effective hurricane monitoring and prediction system. The National Hurricane Center (NHC) in Florida tracks all tropical storm activity in the Atlantic and Eastern Pacific basins because of their potential impact on the Americas. When hurricane strength winds are recorded, the NHC, along with the **National Weather Service's Weather Forecast Offices**, issues a hurricane watch for specific coastal regions to alert people and give them time to prepare.

LICs are often less prepared, because they cannot afford expensive monitoring technology and may not have effective means of communicating information to people likely to be affected.

Protection

Purpose-built storm shelters are often the most reliable way to prevent loss of life during a tropical storm. The shelters have features that make them strong enough to survive tropical storms, such as:

- They may be built off the ground with deep-founded concrete pillars to dissipate energy.
- All windows are covered with metal shutters and don't have glass in them.
- They are often made of strong, reinforced concrete.

High sea walls can also be built in coastal areas to help protect against storm surges.

Planning

Preparation is key to helping reduce the impacts of tropical storms.

- Organisations like the **Red Cross** advise people how to prepare for and respond to an earthquake and its aftermath.
- Countries like Bangladesh have installed early warning systems that have helped to reduce the death toll.
- People in areas at risk of tropical storms are advised to stock up on food and water as they may be unable to safely leave their houses for days at a time.
- Governments implement planning policies that prevent buildings from being constructed in high-risk areas.

(5) Named example

Bangladesh is an LIC in Southern Asia. The country is low-lying, and is therefore particularly vulnerable to tropical storms, but planning schemes have decreased loss of life. These include the installation of an early warning system, and the Emergency Cyclone Recovery and Restoration Project. This project has involved the construction of coastal embankments, and helped to build over 550 storm shelters and repair over 450 existing shelters, to date.

Figure 1 Cyclone shelter in Bangladesh

(5) Worked example   Grade 4

Study **Figure 1**. Explain **one** way this shelter is adapted to reduce the impact of a cyclone.   **[3 marks]**

The cyclone shelter in Figure 1 is built off the ground on concrete pillars, which have deep foundations. The foundations are designed to help dissipate the cyclone's energy, meaning the shelter is less likely to collapse, whilst building the shelter on pillars lifts it above the level of potential storm surges and flooding.

Refer explicitly to the figure or resource you have been asked about. Describe some of its features and why they are significant.

(2) Exam-style practice   Grade 3

Describe **one** way countries can plan for tropical storms.   **[2 marks]**

Made a start   Feeling confident   Exam ready

Weather in the UK

The UK experiences a variety of weather hazards due to the different types of air mass that affect the area.

(5) Five types of extreme weather

1 **Very cold spells** – the coldest temperature on record in the UK was –27.2 °C.

2 **Heatwaves** leading to periods of drought – during the heatwave of summer 2003, the highest temperature ever recorded in the UK was 38.5 °C.

3 **Storms** – these can cause storm surges, coastal flooding, and strong winds and rain that can disrupt travel.

4 **Flash floods** – for example, the 2014 floods in Somerset (**Figure 1**).

5 **Heavy snowfall** – this predominantly affects upland areas such as the Scottish Highlands and the Pennines.

(5) Extreme weather frequency

Rain

Persistent heavy rainfall hits the UK most years. Rivers are increasingly reaching record levels, causing major flooding. Scientists believe climate change will lead to more frequent flooding in the UK on a yearly basis.

Figure 1 Burrowbridge, Somerset, during the 2014 floods

Drought

The UK experiences intermittent periods of drought, especially in southern and eastern England where rainfall levels are comparatively low. For example, in 2016 the Met Office recorded 1294.6 mm of rainfall in the north-west of England, but only 589.9 mm in East Anglia.

Snow

Heavy snowfall has been less frequent in recent years, but extremely cold, blizzard-like conditions have hit the UK in the last 10 years.

(5) Worked example — Grades 1–2

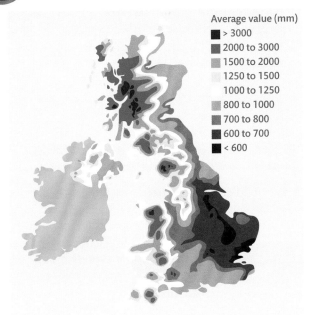

Average value (mm)
- > 3000
- 2000 to 3000
- 1500 to 2000
- 1250 to 1500
- 1000 to 1250
- 800 to 1000
- 700 to 800
- 600 to 700
- < 600

Figure 2 Annual rainfall in the UK 1981–2010

Study **Figure 2**.

State the region of the UK that had the lowest average annual rainfall during this period.

[1 mark]

The south-east of England

Exam focus

When studying a map, take time to familiarise yourself with the information displayed and the associated key.

(5) Exam-style practice — Grades 1–2

Identify **one** type of weather hazard experienced in the UK.

[1 mark]

 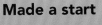

UK extreme weather events

You may be asked to give details about an extreme weather event in the UK that you have studied. This page analyses the causes, impacts and responses to the Somerset flood (2014).

⑤ Named example

Somerset

Weather event: flood, 2014

Initial cause: Heavy downpours of rain (183.8 mm of rain fell in January 2014) caused the River Parrett and the River Tone to flood.

Physical factors: Most of the county of Somerset, in the south-west of England, is on low-lying land which makes it vulnerable to flooding. The county is also bordered to the north by the Bristol channel, which has the second highest tidal range in the world. This can cause floodwater to back up along rivers.

Human factors: The River Parrett and River Tone had not been dredged, which had caused sediment to build up in the channels, reducing the amount of water they could hold.

Key facts:

- It was the most severe flood known to have occurred in Somerset.
- People were trapped in their homes for days at a time, and hundreds had to be evacuated.

Figure 1 Rescue operations in Muchelney, Somerset, during the 2014 floods

⑤ Flood risk management strategies

A new flood defence has been built at Aller Drove, which included raising the level of the road.

A £65–80 million tidal barrier is being built on the River Parrett. — **Flood risk strategies, Somerset** — Temporary pumping sites that drain water have been made permanent.

An 8 km stretch of the River Tone and River Parrett have been dredged to increase their carrying capacity, making them less likely to flood.

⑤ Worked example — Grade 5

Using an example you have studied, explain **two** impacts of an extreme weather event in the UK.

[4 marks]

The Somerset floods of 2014 affected the agricultural industry significantly, with more than 8500 hectares of farmland underwater for 15 days or longer. Additionally, the floods led to disruption of people's daily lives because many roads and bridges were closed due to the floodwaters, which increased commuter time and prevented children from attending school.

⑤ Impacts of the flood

Economic impacts

- It caused significant loss of income for businesses, averaging £17,352 per business in 6 weeks.
- Repairing damage and dredging rivers was very expensive for the government and Somerset County Council; dredging 8 km of river cost around £6 million.

Social impacts

- Many people had an increased commuting time due to road and bridge closures.
- High winds and heavy rainfall led to the loss of power to many homes, with over 600 flooded.
- Hundreds of residents were evacuated.
- Many villages were cut off, which disrupted people's daily lives, including preventing children attending school.

Environmental impacts

- Over 24,000 hectares of farmland, including 63 per cent of winter crop area, were underwater for 15 days or longer.
- Animals and insects drowned, or died from contaminated floodwater or a lack of food.

⑤ Exam-style practice — Grade 4

Describe **two** management strategies that could be used to reduce the risk of flooding in the UK.

[4 marks]

Made a start | Feeling confident | Exam ready

Climate change evidence

Since the start of the Quaternary period, almost 2.6 million years ago, there have been several cycles of glacial advance and retreat. The end of the last Ice Age was about 11,500 years ago.

⑤ Changing global temperatures

Figure 1 shows how the annual global temperature is increasing and provides evidence for **climate change** – this is commonly known as **global warming**. The year 2010 was the warmest year globally since records began in 1880 and some scientists predict that temperatures will continue to rise rapidly. In 2010, the annual global combined land and ocean surface temperature was 0.94 °C above the 20th century average. This was the 39th consecutive year (since 1977) that the yearly global temperature was above average.

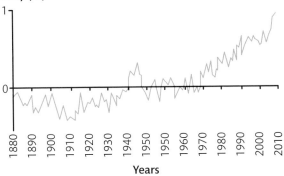

Figure 1 Annual global temperature anomalies from 1880–2010 relative to the 20th-century average (shown by the horizontal axis, at 0)

⑤ Evidence for climate change

Rising sea levels

In the 20th century, global sea levels rose by about 14 cm. They are rising faster now than they were 50 years ago. The world's oceans are warming up, with a 0.1 °C rise in the last century. Scientists believe the rate at which sea levels rise will increase in the future as Arctic ice sheets melt.

Glacial retreat

Scientists believe that glaciers have been retreating at double the rate of any other time in the last 9500 years. The ice in the Himalayas, the Andes, the Alps and the Rockies is retreating at ever greater speeds.

Decreasing ice and snow cover

Recent NASA data has shown a decrease in the size of the ice sheets in Greenland and Antarctica. The extent and thickness of Arctic sea ice has been rapidly declining in recent decades. Monthly September ice extent for 1979 to 2016 declined by 13.3 per cent per decade.

Many places in the northern hemisphere are measuring record-low levels of snow cover in recent years. For example, North America saw three record-low levels of snow between June 2008 and 2012. Eurasia also set a new record-low extent in June of each of those years.

⑤ More evidence for climate change

Pollen analysis, ice cores and tree rings can all provide more evidence for how the Earth's climate has changed over time.

Each plant species produces pollen grains with a unique shape. Therefore, pollen grains preserved in sediment cores allow scientists to determine the abundance and type of vegetation growing when the sediment was deposited. This provides information about what the climate was like during that period.

Ice cores, obtained from drilling deep into ice sheets, contain bubbles of air from when the ice was formed. These bubbles can be sampled to determine the levels of greenhouse gases in the atmosphere at that time.

Tree rings tend to grow wider in warm, wet years and thinner in cold, dry years. By compiling tree ring data, scientists can gather evidence about how the climate has changed over hundreds of years.

⑤ Worked example   Grade 4

Study **Figure 1**. Describe the pattern of global temperature anomalies from 1950–2000.   **[3 marks]**

Between 1950 and 2000, the overall pattern of global temperature anomaly was a consistent increase. Between 1950 and 1970, the temperature anomaly fluctuated a number of times. Some years had very little anomaly, whereas other years had higher temperatures than the 20th-century average. From 1970 to 2000, the anomaly increased steadily, with temperatures rising almost 1°C above the 20th-century average in 2000.

⑤ Exam-style practice   Grade 5

Many scientists believe our climate is changing. Outline the evidence for climate change.   **[4 marks]**

Causes of climate change

Most climate scientists agree that the main cause of global warming is the **greenhouse effect**, which is accelerated by human activity. However, there are also some natural causes that contribute towards climate change.

 Natural causes of climate change

Orbital changes

Milutin Milanković, a geophysicist and astronomer, believed that changes in the Earth's orbit resulted in cyclical variation in the solar radiation reaching the Earth (Milankovitch cycles).

1 The Earth's orbit changes from elliptical (warmer periods) to less elliptical (cooler periods) approximately every 100,000 years.

2 The Earth's tilt on its axis varies between 22.1° and 24.5° over a period of 41,000 years. A larger tilt leads to more extreme seasons, such as warmer summers.

3 Sometimes, the Earth wobbles while spinning, which can affect the severity of the seasons in one hemisphere compared with the other.

Volcanic activity

Volcanic eruptions cause large amounts of sulfur dioxide to be released into the atmosphere.
The sulfur dioxide reacts with other substances to produce sulfate particles, which reflect nearly all radiation, reducing the amount of solar radiation entering the Earth's atmosphere and so causing global cooling. However, volcanic activity can also have the opposite effect; the release of the greenhouse gas carbon dioxide (CO_2) during periods of extreme volcanic activity has caused global warming.

Solar output

Some scientists believe that solar radiation may be a significant cause of increasing global temperatures. However, satellite measurements of solar output since 1978 actually show a slight drop in solar irradiance. Most analysis of longer-term sunspot records indicates that it is unlikely that a change in solar irradiance is the main reason for 20th-century warming.

 Human causes of climate change

Use of fossil fuels

Burning fossil fuels such as coal and oil leads to an increased release of CO_2 into the atmosphere. Scientists believe the rise in the concentration of CO_2 enhances the greenhouse effect.

Deforestation

The clearing and burning of forests leads to a significant rise in the concentration of CO_2 in the atmosphere. This is because the trees no longer absorb CO_2, and the carbon stored in the trees is released into the atmosphere as CO_2 when they are burnt.

Figure 1 Logs ready for transport

Agriculture

The farming of livestock, such as cows, produces methane gas, as do the cultivation methods of crops like rice. Like CO_2, methane is a greenhouse gas and a key contributor towards the greenhouse effect.

 The greenhouse effect

When heat from the Sun is radiated to the Earth, some of it is trapped in the Earth's atmosphere by greenhouse gases, such as water vapour, carbon dioxide and methane, and some of it is reflected back into space. Greenhouse gases maintain the temperature of the Earth making it a habitable environment. As the concentration of greenhouse gases is increasing, more heat is becoming trapped in the Earth's atmosphere, and the temperature of the Earth is rising.

 Worked example   **Grade 5**

Explain **one** natural cause of climate change.

[3 marks]

One natural cause of climate change is variations in the Earth's orbit. Approximately every 100,000 years, the shape of the Earth's orbit changes becoming less elliptical. During this period, the temperatures tend to be cooler.

Other suitable answers would include descriptions of volcanic activity or solar output.

 Exam-style practice   **Grades 1–3**

State **one** human cause of climate change.   **[2 marks]**

Managing climate change

Global climate change has already had severe effects on the environment, including shrinking glaciers, decreasing ice cover, and causing sea levels to rise. Careful management through mitigation and adaptation is essential.

5 Key facts

- Increased temperatures could see a rise in extreme weather events like droughts and flooding, causing significant impacts on freshwater environments and the lives of people who live there.
- An average increase of 1.5 °C could see a 20–30 per cent rise worldwide of species at risk of extinction.
- Rising sea levels could threaten the lives of people living in low-lying coastal areas like in Bangladesh and the Maldives.
- Rising temperatures are likely to cause drought, which will increase the pressure upon water resources.
- Rising sea temperatures are increasing the bleaching of coral reefs, with scientists predicting that by 2050, 98 per cent of reefs around the world will be affected.

Figure 1 Rising sea temperatures have caused coral bleaching in the Caribbean Sea.

10 Mitigation

Alternative energy production

Many countries are looking at renewable energy resources to produce clean energy, for example, solar power, wind energy and hydroelectricity. The state of Tamil Nadu in India now has the world's largest solar power plant, with a capacity of 648 megawatts.

Carbon capture

Carbon capture is a possible solution for reducing the carbon dioxide (CO_2) released when burning fossil fuels. One type of carbon capture involves separating CO_2 from other waste gases at a power plant after a fossil fuel has been burned, then moving it in pipelines to an injection well, where it is injected into the ground and stored.

Planting trees

Planting more trees will help reduce CO_2 levels in the atmosphere. Trees absorb CO_2 during photosynthesis and store it, thus acting as carbon 'sinks'.

International agreements

At the 2015 Paris Agreement, 195 countries signed up to a number of commitments, including contributing towards keeping global temperature increase below 2 °C above pre-industrial temperatures.

10 Adaptation

Agricultural systems

Farmers can adapt their methods to save water and maintain crop yields as temperatures increase. For example, altering the amounts and timing of irrigation using drip feed irrigation systems, using genetically engineered plant crops to increase yields, using drought-resistant crops and alternating growing patterns.

Managing water supply

The increase in extreme weather events like droughts means countries need to ensure they manage water sustainably. Many countries use rainwater capture systems where the use of communal taps can be limited to a certain number of hours during the day.

Reducing risk from rising sea levels

Many low-lying countries like the Maldives and parts of Malaysia have adopted several strategies to try to reduce the risk from rising sea levels. Examples include constructing houses on stilts and restoring coastal mangrove forests.

Other management options include governments passing new laws, restricting what types of building are allowed in coastal areas in order to minimise the number of people at risk from coastal flooding.

2 Exam-style practice   Grade 3

Suggest **one** way humans have adapted to climate change.

[2 marks]

Using examples and case studies

In Papers 1 and 2 you will be expected to use and refer to case studies and named examples that you have learned about.

 Case study question checklist

- ☑ Demonstrate detailed knowledge of the case study, such as the location and the processes involved.
- ☑ Demonstrate your understanding of the interrelationship between the places and processes.

- ☑ Support your points with examples.
- ☑ Use accurate specialist terminology.
- ☑ Produce a balanced argument that looks at both sides and includes a justified conclusion.

You could write about the named example of Typhoon Haiyan or another tropical storm that you have studied.

State which storm you have studied and include specific details, such as dates, location and effects.

 Worked example Grades 5–9

For a tropical storm you have studied, evaluate the effectiveness of the immediate and long-term responses.
[9 marks] [+ 3 SPaG marks]

Typhoon Haiyan started on the 2 November 2013 in the south Pacific Ocean, and quickly became the equivalent of a Category 5 hurricane. Following its aftermath, one of the immediate responses was the provision of emergency survival kits from countries like the UK. These kits provided people with the basic amenities needed for survival, such as food and water, which were distributed with help from the Philippine Red Cross. These survival kits were effective in helping people to recover, but the government required longer-term investment to train people in disaster response. This resulted in the Philippine Red Cross working with the local communities to train people for any future potential disasters.

Another immediate response was the construction of temporary evacuation centres to provide shelter for the 4 million people left homeless. Whilst these shelters were effective in the short term, as they supported vulnerable families whose homes had been destroyed, overcrowding and accessibility created sanitation issues. A year after the storm, officials reported that millions of people were still living in temporary shelters and evacuation centres. Over 200,000 families were reported to be living in areas deemed unsafe by the government, due to the lack of available land to re-house people. Therefore, the long-term government response to the number of homes destroyed by the typhoon was arguably ineffective and inadequate. Other long-term responses also included NGOs, such as Oxfam, working to help rebuild people's houses and restore their means of making a living. The area affected by the typhoon included a number of farming and fishing communities, and many fishing boats and coconut plantations were severely damaged by the storm. Oxfam helped to repair boats, used fallen trees to rebuild houses, and provided hundreds of tons of rice seed, to help secure both food and income for people affected by the typhoon.

To conclude, immediate responses to Typhoon Haiyan by other countries, NGOs and the Philippine government were widespread, co-ordinated and effective, as they provided for people's short-term needs, such as shelter, food and water. However, although long-term responses by NGOs helped to restore the local economy and create a secure food supply, the rebuilding effort did not adequately address the number of people displaced by the storm. This is shown by the fact that one year on, there were still more than 5000 families living in temporary shelters, which increased their vulnerability to the effects of any subsequent tropical storms...

Write a clear and concise conclusion summarising your main points and include a balanced judgement about the effectiveness of both types of response in relation to the example you have chosen.

 Exam-style practice Grades 5–9

For **two** earthquakes or volcanic eruptions you have studied, evaluate and compare the effectiveness of the immediate and long-term responses.
[9 marks] [+ 3 SPaG marks]

 Made a start Feeling confident ☑ Exam ready

A small-scale ecosystem

You need to know the key components of a small-scale ecosystem in the UK and how these components interact. This page will look at a pond, which is a freshwater aquatic ecosystem.

⑤ What is an ecosystem?

An ecosystem is a geographical area consisting of plants, animals and other organisms, which interact together.

Ecosystems contain both biotic and abiotic components:

❶ Biotic components are all the living organisms in an ecosystem.

❷ Abiotic components are all the non-living things, such as soil type and air temperature.

Ecosystems can be very small, like a pond or hedgerow ecosystem, or very large, like a tropical rainforest. A very large ecosystem is called a **global ecosystem**.

Named example

Frensham Little Pond in Surrey is an example of a small-scale ecosystem. It is a Site of Special Scientific Interest because this special habitat is home to rare wildlife.

⑤ Ecosystem key terms

- ⊘ **Producers** are organisms that produce their own food through converting the Sun's energy.
- ⊘ **Consumers** are organisms that generate energy from feeding on other organisms.
- ⊘ **Decomposers** are fungi and bacteria that break down organic material.
- ⊘ **Food chains** show how energy flows from producers to consumers and then to decomposers.
- ⊘ **Food webs** show how all the food chains in a particular ecosystem interact.
- ⊘ **Nutrient cycles** show how nutrients move from the environment into living organisms and are recycled back into the environment.

⑩ A pond ecosystem

- Producers in a pond ecosystem include plants, such as pickleweed, algae, and water lilies.
- Some ponds also have species of plants growing around their edge, such as reeds and bulrushes, which are also producers. These tall plants provide a nesting habitat for water birds like ducks and moorhens.
- Herbivores in pond ecosystems are often insects, such as pond snails and water beetles.
- Carnivores include fish, such as pike, as well as herons and frogs.
- Abiotic factors affect pond ecosystems. Very cold temperatures can cause a pond to freeze, harming or killing the organisms living in it. Very hot temperatures reduce the amount of oxygen the water can hold, so less is available for respiration.

If the population of carnivores, such as frogs, decreases, the population of their prey, the herbivores, is likely to increase rapidly. This will put pressure on the producers.

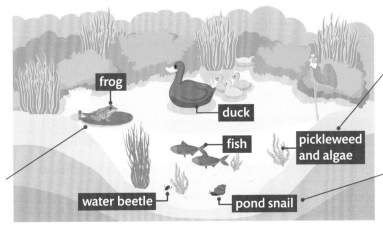

If the oxygen level in the pond decreases, producers, such as pickleweed and algae, may not survive. This means there may not be enough food for herbivores which feed on them.

If the population of herbivores, such as pond snails, decreases, there may not be enough food for all the carnivores, such as fish and ducks, which feed on them. This may impact the carnivore population.

Figure 1 Organisms in a pond ecosystem

⑤ Exam-style practice Grade 4

Using an example that you have studied, describe what might happen to the carnivore population in a small-scale ecosystem if the population of herbivores rapidly decreased. **[4 marks]**

Tropical rainforests

Tropical rainforests are distinctive biomes with a hugely diverse range of plant and animal species. They occur within or near the tropics and they cover approximately 7 per cent of the Earth's land surface.

⑤ Key characteristics

- ☑ The climate is hot and humid all year round, with average daily temperatures of 28 °C.
- ☑ Rainfall is high, with nearly daily downpours typically adding up to over 2000 mm per year.
- ☑ Heavy rainfall leaches nutrients from the soil so the main source of nutrients is decomposing plants and animals on the forest floor.
- ☑ Rainforests have very high levels of biodiversity.
- ☑ Local tribes use food and resources sustainably and live in harmony with the environment.

② Location

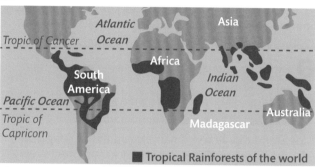

Figure 1 The main areas of tropical rainforest are in South and Central America, West Africa and Indonesia.

⑩ Rainforest vegetation

The emergent layer
This is formed by the tops of the tallest and strongest trees which reach above the rainforest canopy. Trees here are exposed to the most sunlight of any of the layers of vegetation.

The canopy
This layer is exposed to the sunlight and provides shade below. It is generally 20–40 m tall, so some trees have buttress roots to provide stability. The canopy is full of birds, insects, frogs and animals such as sloths and monkeys.

The under canopy
More sunlight reaches the under canopy than the shrub level, but it is still shady. It contains saplings of trees waiting for a gap in the canopy to grow into, and woody climbing plants called lianas, which wind themselves around trees to grow up towards the sunlight. Some trees have drip-tip leaves to allow heavy rain to run off quickly, rather than damage the plant.

The shrub level
This is the ground layer near the forest floor. The Sun is blocked out by taller trees, so not much vegetation survives.

Figure 2 Tropical rainforests have different levels of vegetation.

⑤ Worked example Grade 5

Explain how **two** species of animal have adapted to surviving in tropical rainforests. **[4 marks]**

Three-toed sloths have very long claws that help them climb and hang from branches in the rainforest canopy. They have an extra neck vertebrae that allows them to turn their heads 270°, which helps them to see their predators, such as jaguars, more easily. The Sumatran tiger has webbing between its toes to help it swim, allowing it to cross the many rivers that run through its forest habitat in Sumatra.

⑤ Exam-style practice Grades 3–5

Describe the distribution of tropical rainforests. **[3 marks]**

Deforestation in Indonesia

You may need to answer a question about deforestation using a case study that you have studied. This case study looks at the causes and impacts of deforestation in Indonesia.

 Case study

Indonesia

Indonesia is located in South-East Asia, between the *Indian Ocean* and the *Pacific Ocean*. It is one of the most important areas of tropical rainforest in the world, but deforestation is a serious problem. In 2000, 85 per cent of Indonesia was covered by trees, but since then huge areas of forest have been destroyed.

The annual rate of deforestation varies. It was highest in 2012, when over 840,000 hectares of trees were cut down, the most forest lost by any country in the world that year. The lowest rate was in 2003, when only 230,000 hectares of forest were cleared.

Although the average rate of deforestation decreased significantly in 2013, it rose again in 2014, and the general trend in the years 2000–2015 has been a steady increase in the rate of deforestation.

Figure 1 Among other things, the rainforest in Indonesia is home to at least 500 mammal species and 40,000 plant species.

Causes

- **Logging** – poorer local people can earn far more from logging than from farming.
- **Gold and copper mining** – forests are cleared for mines and the roads that lead to them.
- **Road building** – roads are built through the forest to transport resources, such as gold and timber.
- **Commercial plantations** – large areas of forest are cleared for plantations, such as for palm oil.
- **Subsistence farming** (where people farm to produce enough only to feed themselves and their families) – farmers cut or burn down forest to clear land for farming.
- **Construction of hydroelectric dams**
- **Population growth and settlement** – Indonesia's population has grown rapidly from around 87 million in 1960 to nearly 258 million in 2015. Forests have been cleared to provide land to build houses on.

Impacts

👎 Loss of rainforest habitat for the thousands of species.

👎 Local people have been exploited by mining or logging companies, often having to work in dangerous conditions for low wages.

👎 Deforestation increases soil erosion as there are no trees to protect the soil from the heavy tropical rain, leading to greater surface run-off and flooding.

👎 Carbon dioxide is released when trees are felled or burned, which increases greenhouse gas emissions.

👍 Valuable exports, such as gold, copper and palm oil, bring in a lot of money, which has helped Indonesia to develop its economy very quickly – it is now the sixteenth largest economy in the world.

👍 Investment in renewable energy, such as hydroelectric dams, will help Indonesia provide energy for its growing population and decrease its reliance on fossil fuels.

There have also been violent conflicts between private companies and local people trying to protect their forest.

The increasing rate of deforestation in Indonesia has resulted in the country becoming one of the biggest emitters of greenhouse gases.

The command word 'describe' means you need to refer to specific points, and 'explain' means you need to give reasons. Include specific details from your tropical rainforest case study to show your knowledge and support your points.

Exam-style practice   **Grades 5–7**

Describe and explain the impacts of deforestation on **one** tropical rainforest you have studied.   **[6 marks]**

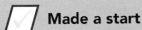

Sustainable rainforests

Sustainable management of tropical rainforests is vital to protect their biodiversity.

 15 Rainforest management strategies

Rainforest management strategies are essential to slow the increasing rates of deforestation, particularly in Indonesia and South America.

Selective logging and replanting

- Selective logging is the practice of cutting down trees when they are over a certain height, and only harvesting one or two species of tree in an area of forest. The Indonesian government is working with non-governmental organisations (NGOs), like the World Wide Fund for Nature (WWF), and international organisations to promote the trading of timber from legally verified sources.
- In Sumatra, Indonesia, millions of trees are being replanted to restore animal habitats that have been lost due to palm oil production.

International agreements

- In 2006, the International Tropical Timber Agreement was established, supported by the United Nations (UN).
- The main aim of the agreement was to promote the global trade of tropical timber (including hardwoods) from sustainably managed forests. Sustainability is defined by the UN as 'development that meets the needs of the present without compromising the ability of future generations to meet their own needs'.

Conservation and education

- The WWF works closely with stakeholders to help conserve the world's rainforests. One strategy has been campaigning for the creation of national parks to protect the diverse range of plant and animal species.
- The WWF also promotes sustainable production of wood products through an initiative called the Global Forest and Trade Network.
- A powerful incentive is debt reduction, where some of a country's debt is written off in return for commitments to protect their rainforest.
- Working with local communities to ensure they can make a sustainable living from the rainforest is essential to its protection. A successful example is Brazil nut production, in Bolivia. The Bolivian government protects the rainforest because a healthy forest is needed to produce a good crop and the industry employs over 20,000 people.

Ecotourism

- In Borneo, in South-East Asia, soft trekking – where tourists walk through specifically designated trails – helps to preserve the plants and wildlife species.
- Huts for small tour groups can be built from locally sourced timber, providing a source of income for the local communities.
- Trekking guides can be hired by tourists, which provides an income for local people.

> Strategies such as the development of ecotourism and working with local communities are very important. They provide a powerful incentive to local people to protect the rainforest by helping them to make a living from it. This can combat causes of deforestation such as clearing forested land for subsistence farming.

> You can save time by writing an abbreviation like the one for non-governmental organisations in the worked example.

 5 Worked example   **Grade 4**

Suggest **one** way non-governmental organisations can help to manage tropical rainforests in a more sustainable way. **[2 marks]**

NGOs can work with governments and international organisations to implement initiatives that promote sustainable development. An example is promoting the trade of sustainably sourced timber.

 5 Exam-style practice   **Grade 5**

Explain how tropical rainforests can be managed sustainably. **[4 marks]**

     Made a start   **Feeling confident**   **Exam ready**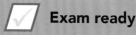

Characteristics of hot deserts

Hot deserts are primarily located in belts along the lines of 30°N and 30°S latitude and are known for their hostile and challenging conditions. The largest desert in the world is the Sahara in northern Africa.

② Location of hot deserts

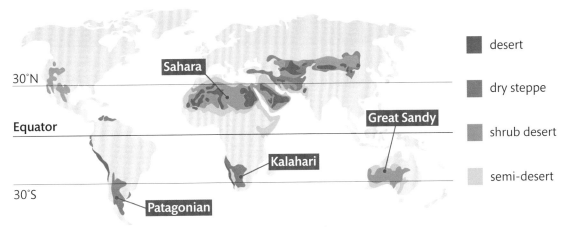

Figure 1 Deserts cover approximately 20 per cent of the Earth's land surface.

⑤ Key characteristics

- ✓ Hot deserts usually have less than 250 mm of rainfall per year.
- ✓ The climate during the day is hot and dry, with some locations recording temperatures above 50°C, but temperatures can get very cold at night, sometimes falling below 0°C.
- ✓ Freshwater oases, which act as biodiversity hotspots rich in rare plants and animals, are being threatened by warming temperatures, less predictable rainfall and habitat degradation.

⑤ Animal adaptations

- Owls and bats are only active at night when the temperatures are much lower.
- Lizards and snakes are only active during the early morning before finding shelter from the Sun under sand and rocks.
- Camels conserve water by sweating as little as possible, and have a fatty hump so that their energy store doesn't insulate their whole body and cause them to overheat.

⑤ Plant adaptations

Figure 2 Giant Saguaros in West Tucson, Arizona, USA

- Cacti are xerophytes, which can store water and have no leaves in order to reduce transpiration.
- Desert lilies have a very short reproductive life cycle. They bloom vigorously for a few weeks in the spring after rain has fallen and lie dormant for the rest of the year. Their bulbs and seeds are heat and drought resistant, too.
- Phreatophyte plants have long roots, enabling them to draw water directly from the water table.

⑤ Worked example | Grade 5

Explain **two** ways plants have adapted to survive in hot deserts. **[4 marks]**

Plants, such as cacti, have adapted to survive in hot deserts by having no leaves, which reduces transpiration and allows them to store water.

Some plants, such as the desert lily, have adapted their behaviour so that they lie dormant during the hottest seasons, and then rejuvenate during the spring. This enables them to capture the water they need before going back into a dormant state.

⑤ Exam-style practice | Grades 3–5

❶ State **one** characteristic of hot deserts. **[1 mark]**
❷ Describe the distribution of hot deserts. **[3 marks]**

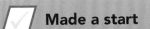 **Made a start** | **Feeling confident** | **Exam ready** | **23**

Opportunities and challenges in a hot desert

You may need to answer a question about opportunities and challenges in a hot desert using a case study that you have studied. This case study looks at the Sahara.

Case study

The Sahara

Over 50 per cent of the Sahara receives less than 26 mm of rain per year. When rainfall occurs, it normally does so in heavy torrential downpours.

It is home to a range of plant and animal species, including the deathstalker scorpion, but biodiversity levels are low, mainly due to the extreme conditions. Plants and animals need to be highly adapted to survive in the challenging conditions. For more about adaptations, go to page 23.

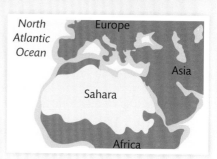

Figure 1 The Sahara is the world's largest hot desert. It stretches across northern Africa and covers approximately 9 million square kilometres.

Opportunites

Economy
The oil and gas sector is vital for the economy of countries like Algeria, accounting for 35 per cent of its total gross domestic product (GDP).

Tourism
There are camel trekking and 4×4 tours around Erg Chebbi, Morocco.

 Development opportunities

Solar energy
Morocco is building the Noor 1 solar power plant, which will be the largest in the world, capable of producing an estimated 580 megawatts of energy.

Farming
The soil is mainly infertile with most farming being subsistence farming. The main commercial crops are dates and fruit.

Mineral extraction
Key minerals like limestone, copper and phosphate are found in the Sahara.

 Challenges

1 **Extreme temperatures** – the Sahara is one of the driest places on Earth, with a mean temperature of 30 °C, and temperatures reaching up to 50 °C during the summer.

2 **Water scarcity and drought** – these threaten life, livelihoods and food security.

3 **Inaccessibility** – the Sahara's harsh rocky landscape of mountains and plateaus makes the construction of infrastructure difficult.

Worked example  Grades 4–5

Explain **one** way in which hot deserts provide opportunities. **[3 marks]**

Hot deserts provide an opportunity for mineral extraction, which creates jobs for locals and generates income for the economy. For example, the Sahara has an abundance of minerals like copper.

You could write about other opportunities including farming, energy and tourism that are specific to the case study you have studied.

Exam-style practice Grades 5–8

Discuss how hot deserts can create both opportunities and challenges. **[6 marks]**

 Made a start 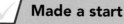 Feeling confident 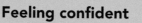 Exam ready

Desertification

Desertification is the process of fertile land turning into a desert over time. Areas on the edge of hot deserts are particularly at risk of desertification.

⏱ Causes of desertification

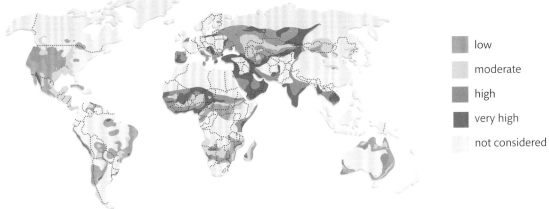

- low
- moderate
- high
- very high
- not considered

Figure 1 A map showing the level of risk of desertification induced by human activity. Desertification tends to occur on the edge of existing deserts.

- **Overgrazing** – the intensive grazing of land by animals leads to the soil becoming bare, compacted and prone to drying out and cracking.
- **Over-cultivation** – the intensive growing of crops to meet the demands of a growing population, without giving the land a chance to recover, causes the soil to become infertile, exposed and vulnerable to erosion.
- **Population growth** – rising population puts pressure on demands for resources.
- **Removal of fuel wood** – cutting down trees to use the wood for fuel causes the roots to die, removing the binding agent for the soil.
- **Climate change** – hotter and drier conditions are increasing the susceptibility of land to desertification.

⏱ Management strategies

- **Water and soil management** – appropriate planting and harvesting of crops ensures the soil can recover. The use of water can be managed using small-scale irrigation projects, such as catching and storing rainwater and using sprinklers to irrigate farmland.
- **Tree planting** – this helps to reduce soil erosion as the tree roots help to stabilise the soil structure.
- **Appropriate technology** – this involves the use of technology (or techniques) that can be easily repaired or replicated by locals. An example is the use of rocks to create small walls around farmers' fields to trap water, helping to increase crop production and yields.

Exam focus
Not all questions indicate how many points you should include. You should be guided by the number of marks. For example, this question is worth four marks, so you should provide two causes with thorough explanations.

⏱ Worked example · Grade 5

Explain the causes of desertification.

[4 marks]

One of the causes of desertification is the over-cultivation of land due to rising populations. This means that farmers intensively farm the same piece of land continuously, not allowing the soil time to recover. This over-cultivation strips nutrients from the soil, leaving it infertile and limiting plant growth. The lack of plant cover means that the soil is then easily eroded by the wind and rain.

Another cause of desertification is trees being cut down to be used for fuel wood. The tree roots, which had held the soil together, die and the soil becomes loose. The soil can again easily be blown or washed away.

⏱ Exam-style practice · Grade 5

Explain how the rate of desertification can be reduced.

[4 marks]

Characteristics of cold environments

The cold environments of the Arctic tundra and polar regions are some of the most extreme places on Earth, in which the climate, soils, plants, animals and people interact and depend on each other for survival.

Key facts

- The **Arctic tundra** and the **polar regions** are some of the coldest places on Earth, with average winter temperatures ranging from −40 °C in the Arctic tundra to −60 °C at the South Pole.
- Many animal species, such as wolves, musk ox and Arctic foxes, live in the Arctic tundra. The musk ox is adapted for survival with powerful hooves that can break the ice to access the water underneath for drinking, and thick fur to keep it warm.
- The polar regions are home to animal species such as seals, whales, polar bears and penguins. Seals and whales are adapted to keep warm in the freezing water with a thick layer of fat (blubber). Polar bears also have a thick layer of fat, up to 11 cm thick.
- The Antarctic ice sheet covers about 98 per cent of Antarctica.
- Plants are highly adapted to the extreme conditions, which include soil that is frozen for most of the year. Arctic moss grows in lakes and bogs where it can store nutrients in its leaves. Snow saxifrage grows close to the ground to reduce potential damage from the wind and ice.

Interdependence

Plants and lichens have adapted to the extreme temperatures, by growing quickly in spring when temperatures rise. They provide a habitat for ground-nesting birds, like geese, and are food for herbivores, such as reindeer and hares. These herbivores are hunted by wolves, bears and foxes, which are adapted to the extreme cold with thick layers of fur. Indigenous people living in cold environments, such as the Inuit in Greenland and Athabascan in Alaska, rely on these animals for food, tools and clothing.

Biodiversity

Biodiversity in cold environments is low. This is because the extreme cold and low levels of precipitation make it difficult for organisms to survive. These conditions also mean that decomposition is slow, so soils are generally thin and infertile; this limits the plant species which can grow. Biodiversity does increase in summer, when hours of sunlight and temperatures increase and migratory animals and birds arrive. However, the ecosystem is fragile, and any changes can have an impact on the whole food web.

Worked example   Grade 5

Study **Figure 1**. Explain **two** ways the Arctic fox is adapted to cold environments.   **[4 marks]**

One way the Arctic fox is adapted to cold environments is its thick fur coat, which changes colour from brown-grey in summer to white in winter. This insulates it against the cold and helps to keep it camouflaged all year round, making it easier for it to hunt small mammals such as hares. The Arctic fox also has a very thick tail, which it uses to help it balance and to wrap around itself as protection against the wind and cold.

Figure 1 An Arctic fox in winter

Exam-style practice   Grades 1–4

1 State **one** characteristic of the Arctic tundra biome.   **[1 mark]**

2 Explain **one** way plants have adapted to cold environments.   **[2 marks]**

Opportunities and challenges in tundra

You may need to answer a question about development in cold environments using a case study that you have studied. This case study looks at the opportunities and challenges of development in the Siberian tundra in the north-east of Russia.

⑤ Case study

Siberia
In Siberia, winters can be extremely cold, with temperatures plummeting to –60 °C.

The Siberian tundra has two soil layers:

- **Permafrost** is permanently frozen ground that occurs when soil temperatures remain below 0 °C for a minimum of two years.
- The **active layer** lies above the permafrost. It freezes and thaws and is greater in depth in the summer.

⑤ Development opportunities in Siberia

The **oil fields** in Western Siberia provide approximately 70 per cent of Russia's oil production.

Siberia has the potential to develop its use of **biomass energy** with the Kamchatka Peninsula region potentially able to produce 2 GW of energy.

Siberia covers a vast area and includes many rivers and the largest and deepest lake in the world, Lake Baikal. This offers huge opportunities for **commercial fishing** and fish farming, as well as attracting tourists to the area specifically to fish.

Development opportunities

Despite the cold temperatures, the short summers provide opportunities to harness **solar energy**. In Siberia's Altai Republic, the Kosh-Agachskaya plant is one of five planned for the region.

Tourism in the Siberian tundra is increasing with walking tours, sea cruises, skiing and rafting available. One of the key tourist destinations is the Russian Arctic National Park with attractions including the wooden House of Eira.

Siberia has an abundance of **minerals** including gold, nickel, silver and zinc. Norilsk Nickel plant is one of the biggest for nickel-mining in the region.

⑤ Challenges

1. **Extreme temperatures** – with winter temperatures reaching –60 °C, warm thermal clothing is essential. Traditional tribes, like the Nenets, wear reindeer skin as an insulator.
2. **Inaccessibility** – many parts of Siberia are extremely remote, with transport links limited. Some people use snowmobiles, while the Nenets use their reindeer.
3. **Provision of buildings and infrastructure** – the melting of the active layer every summer means buildings need to be specially adapted to avoid being flooded. Yakutsk, in the Sakha Republic, has buildings that are supported on concrete and stilts to protect them when the active layer of soil melts.

⑤ Worked example   Grades 3–5

Describe **one** development opportunity in cold environments.   **[3 marks]**

Siberia, Russia, is a cold environment that provides opportunities for the extraction of minerals like gold and nickel. The Norilsk Nickel plant provides employment and boosts the local economy with the sale of the resource to a global market. Higher temperatures due to global warming may make it easier to extract these minerals, helping to improve this development opportunity further.

⑤ Exam-style practice   Grade 5

Explain how the development of cold environments can provide challenges for people.   **[4 marks]**

✓ **Made a start**   ✓ **Feeling confident**   ✓ **Exam ready**

Conservation of cold environments

Cold environments, like the tundra, are extremely fragile environments. It is vital to ensure that economic development of the area is not at the expense of the environment.

 Importance of cold environments

Cold environments have value as wilderness areas; wild places which have not been changed by human activity. Animals and plants have evolved to adapt to the extreme conditions in the Arctic. Many species would struggle to survive increases in temperature or air pollution.

Figure 1 Oil spills have polluted rivers and nearby land in Siberia, harming plant and wildlife species.

Indigenous tribes rely on these landscapes for survival, and rely upon the animals that live there for their food, clothing and tools. Development could harm their traditional way of life.

Preventing ice sheets and glaciers in Arctic areas from melting is essential for helping to stop the global rise in sea levels.

 Methods of management

Use of technology

The construction of oil pipelines can have significant impacts on the environment. The designers of the Trans-Alaska Pipeline adapted their design to minimise these impacts. For example, the pipeline is raised off the ground on stilts to prevent it from melting the permafrost and to allow wildlife species to continue to migrate across the landscape.

International agreements

The Antarctic Treaty was signed in 1959 by 12 countries that had territorial claims over Antarctica. The treaty was established to ensure that the environment was protected. It includes a series of agreements to ensure that any activities, like scientific research and tourism, are monitored and regulated.

Role of governments

The Strategic Action Program for Protection of the Russian Arctic Environment (SAP-Arctic) was set up with the main aim of ensuring the preservation and protection of the Arctic environment from economic activities.

Conservation groups

In 1992, the WWF implemented its Arctic Programme with the main aims of maintaining the fragile environment, protecting wildlife and promoting the sustainable use of resources. The WWF works with local stakeholders and the media to raise awareness of the most important threats and opportunities faced by the natural environment. They also assist in the implementation of strategies to protect it.

 Worked example | **Grades 5–6**

Outline **two** reasons why cold environments need to be managed. **[4 marks]**

One reason is because many of them are home to traditional indigenous tribes. Economic development of these landscapes can lead to irreversible changes that can threaten the survival of these tribes. For example, the pollution of water supplies from oil extraction reduces availability of water. Furthermore, many of these landscapes provide habitats for plant and wildlife species, which can be damaged by development or the extraction of resources. For example, oil pipelines can restrict migration pathways and the warm oil in the pipelines can thaw the permafrost and cause the pipeline to sink, break and leak.

Exam-style practice | **Grades 5–6**

Explain how cold environments can be managed by different stakeholders. **[4 marks]**

 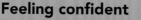

Landscapes in the UK

In Paper 1, Section C, you will have to answer two questions on landscapes in the UK from a choice of three – coastal, river and glacial landscapes. All three topics are covered in the next few pages, but you can focus your revision on the two you have studied in class.

(10) Location and features of UK upland and lowland areas

Upland landscapes are areas of land high above sea level, which are often hilly or mountainous. Lowland areas are much closer to sea level, and often have wide flat plains and fertile soils. You need to know the location of the major upland and lowland areas and the main river systems in the UK.

The Highlands of Scotland are one of the main upland areas in the UK. They are a rugged mountainous landscape with areas of steep relief, hard, resistant rock such as granite, and the UK's highest mountain, Ben Nevis (1345 m).

Most of the upland areas in the UK are in the north west. Many of them are National Parks, including the Lake District, Snowdonia, and the Peak District.

There are also some upland landscapes in the south west of the UK, including Dartmoor in Devon.

Height of land above sea level (metres)
- >800
- 400–800
- 150–399
- 50–149
- 0–49

Lowland landscapes often have fertile soils and gentle relief, so are suitable for arable and pastoral farming. Upland areas are often only suitable for sheep farming, as they tend to have thin, infertile soils and many areas of steep relief.

The Norfolk Broads in East Anglia are a lowland landscape. They are flat and very close to sea level. The highest point is only 38 m above sea level.

Lowland landscapes in the south east are mostly made of sedimentary rock, such as the white cliffs of Dover, which are made of chalk.

Figure 1 Map of the UK showing relief

(5) The longest UK rivers

- The River Severn (354 km) in the west of the UK, flows from Wales into the Severn Estuary in England.
- The River Thames (346 km), in the south east of the UK, runs through the middle of London.
- The River Trent (297 km) runs from the West Midlands to the north east.
- The River Great Ouse (230 km) flows from central England to the coast of East Anglia.
- The River Wye (215 km) in the west, flows from Wales into the Severn Estuary.

(2) Worked example — Grades 1–3

Which **two** of the following statements are true?
Shade **two** circles only. **[2 marks]**

A The River Thames is the longest river in the UK. ○

B Two of the five longest rivers in the UK flow into the Severn Estuary. ◉

C Three of the UK's five longest rivers have their source in Wales. ○

D Only two rivers in the UK are over 300 km long. ◉

(5) Exam-style practice — Grades 3–4

Study **Figure 1**. Describe the distribution of upland landscapes in the UK. **[4 marks]**

Waves and weathering

Constructive and destructive waves are a key driving force in the dynamic nature of our coasts. Alongside this, the interaction of weathering processes contributes towards constantly changing environments.

 Types of wave

Coastal landscapes are shaped by the power of waves; these are created by wind blowing over the sea surface, both locally and distantly. The size and energy of a wave is determined by:

- how far the wave has travelled (the **fetch**)
- the power of the wind and how long (in time) the wind has been blowing.

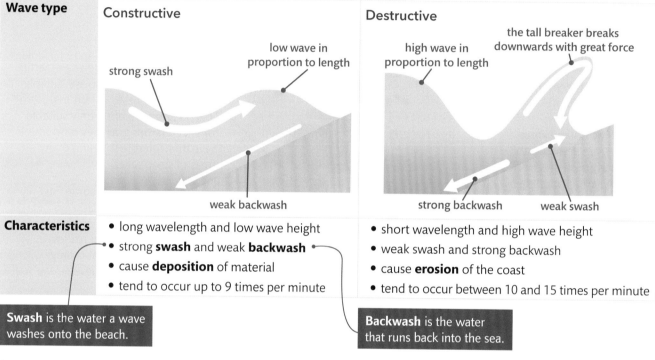

Wave type	Constructive	Destructive
	strong swash / low wave in proportion to length / weak backwash	high wave in proportion to length / the tall breaker breaks downwards with great force / strong backwash / weak swash
Characteristics	• long wavelength and low wave height • strong **swash** and weak **backwash** • cause **deposition** of material • tend to occur up to 9 times per minute	• short wavelength and high wave height • weak swash and strong backwash • cause **erosion** of the coast • tend to occur between 10 and 15 times per minute

Swash is the water a wave washes onto the beach.

Backwash is the water that runs back into the sea.

 Types of weathering

Chemical weathering

When acidic rainwater falls on rocks, a chemical reaction can occur. Over time, this can cause the breakdown of certain rocks like limestone.

Mechanical weathering

This includes several different physical processes of weathering, including cracking caused by expansion and contraction of rocks as they heat up and cool down, the breakdown of trees by rocks (biological weathering), and **freeze-thaw weathering**.

Freeze-thaw weathering is a process in which rainwater falls into the cracks of rocks and freezes. This causes the water to expand, putting pressure on the rock. Repeated freezing and thawing causes the breakdown of rocks over time.

 Worked example Grades 1–2

Which **one** of the following statements describes the process of chemical weathering? Shade **one** circle only. **[1 mark]**

A the breakdown of rocks due to the acidity of rainwater ⬤

B the breakdown of rocks due to the roots of vegetation ◯

C the breakdown of rocks due to water freezing in cracks ◯

Only **A** describes a chemical process, so this must be the correct answer.

 Exam-style practice Grades 2–3

1 State **one** characteristic of constructive waves. **[1 mark]**

2 Explain how freeze-thaw weathering breaks rocks over time. **[2 marks]**

 Made a start   **Feeling confident**   **Exam ready**

Coastal erosion landforms

Coastal erosion processes interact to form distinctive landforms like headlands and bays, cliffs and wave cut platforms, caves, arches and stacks.

⑤ Coastal processes of erosion

- **Hydraulic power** (Mechanical) – breaking waves compress pockets of air in cracks in a cliff. The increasing air pressure causes the cracks to widen, which leads to rocks breaking off.
- **Abrasion** (Mechanical) – this is the action of rock fragments carried by waves being hurled at a cliff face, causing pieces of rock to chip off.
- **Attrition** (Mechanical) – waves cause rocks and pebbles to collide with each other, causing them to become smaller and rounded.
- **Solution/Corrosion** (Chemical) – acids and salts in seawater cause some rocks to gradually dissolve.

⑤ Cliffs and wave cut platforms

1. Waves crashing against a cliff will, over time, lead to the formation of a **wave cut notch** through erosional processes like abrasion.
2. Continued erosion will cause the notch to increase in size, creating an **overhang**.
3. Eventually, the overhang will be unable to support itself and will collapse under the force of gravity.
4. Repetition of this sequence will cause the formation of a **wave cut platform**.

⑤ Caves, arches and stacks

There are four stages in the formation of a stack.

1. Waves attack **faults** (cracks or areas of weakness) on a headland through processes of erosion such as hydraulic power.
2. Over time, these areas of weakness increase in size to form a small **cave**.
3. If two caves form either side of the headland, eventually erosion will cause the backs of the caves to meet and break through, forming an **arch**.
4. The neck of the arch widens with additional erosion. This, along with weathering on the top, results in the arch collapsing, forming a **stack**. If a stack collapses it will leave a **stump**.

For this question, you could have alternatively given abrasion or corrosion.

② Headlands and bays

Coastlines can be made up of alternating bands of hard, resistant rocks like granite, and soft, less resistant rocks like clay. **Bays** are formed when the bands of less resistant rock erode. This leaves behind a band of more resistant rock jutting out into the sea. These are called **headlands**. Headlands are more vulnerable to erosion because wave energy is concentrated there.

② Worked example — Grades 1–3

Figure 1 The beach, headland and arch at Durdle Door, Dorset

Study **Figure 1**.
State **one** process of erosion that may affect this arch. **[1 mark]**

Hydraulic power

Named example
Durdle Door is an example of coastal erosion in the UK. The arch will eventually collapse to leave a stack.

⑩ Exam-style practice — Grades 4–7

1. Using **Figure 1**, explain the processes involved in the formation of an arch. **[6 marks]**
2. Explain how **one** erosional process is involved in smoothing and shaping a wave cut platform. **[2 marks]**

Mass movement and transportation

Surface materials move down a slope under the influence of gravity. This is known as **mass movement**. When mass movement occurs along coastlines, this material is often transported further along the coast by the process of **longshore drift**.

(10) Types of mass movement

Sliding

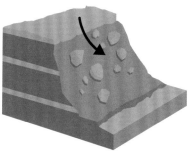

This is the sudden movement of large volumes of rock and soil along a zone of saturated soil.

Slumping

This is the rapid mass movement of permeable rock and soil such as clay, which has become heavily saturated, lying on top of impermeable material.

Rock falls

This is the free-fall movement of rock fragments due to gravity. This process is often increased by mechanical weathering.

Figure 1 Three types of mass movement

(5) Transport processes

Solution
dissolved minerals carried within the water

Traction
the rolling of large pebbles along the sea floor

Transport processes

Suspension
particles carried within the water

Saltation
the bouncing of small pebbles along the sea floor

(2) Longshore drift

Longshore drift is the gradual movement of sediment along the coast. The direction of the prevailing wind causes the waves to approach the beach at an oblique angle (swash) and return at a right angle (backwash). This causes sediment to be carried along the coast in a zigzag.

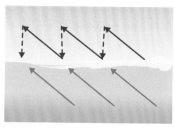

-- backwash
— swash
— prevailing wind

Figure 2 Longshore drift

(5) Worked example — Grade 5

Explain how sediment is transported along coastlines.

[4 marks]

Sediment is transported by the process of longshore drift. The swash of waves brings sediment onto the beach at an angle determined by the prevailing wind. Much of the sediment is dragged back into the sea by the backwash at a 90° angle to the coast. This process continues and, over time, this results in the sediment being transported along the coastline until it reaches a form of coastal management or a change in the shape of the coastline.

Give specific details about the process you are explaining.

Use relevant key terms in your explanation.

(5) Exam-style practice — Grades 2–4

1 State **one** type of mass movement. **[1 mark]**

2 Describe **one** way slumping affects coastal landscapes. **[2 marks]**

Made a start   Feeling confident   Exam ready

Coastal deposition landforms

Coastal deposition is the process of sediment being deposited by waves. It leads to the formation of landforms, such as spits and bars, sand dunes and beaches.

 Formation of spits and bars

Formation of spits
A **spit** is a narrow accumulation of sand and shingle formed by longshore drift, which is caused by the prevailing wind blowing at an angle to the coastline. One end of a spit is connected to land and the other end projects out into the sea.

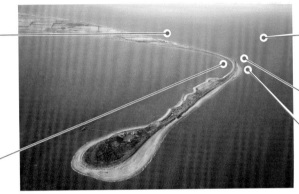

1. Spits form from the transportation of sediment to the end of a coastline by **longshore drift**.

4. A **salt marsh** forms from the build-up of deposited sediments behind the spit.

Named example
Spurn Head in East Yorkshire is affected by longshore drift and is an example of a spit.

2. The sediment is then deposited out at sea and accumulates to form a spit over time.

3. Strong **secondary winds** cause the end of the spit to curve.

Figure 1 Spurn Head, East Yorkshire

Formation of bars
A bar forms if a spit extends across a bay, connecting to a headland on the other side. This results in the formation of a **lagoon**, which is a saltwater lake.

 Formation of sand dunes

1 Onshore winds cause **sand dunes** to form at the back of a beach.

2 Initially, sand is deposited around an obstruction, such as a rock, forming embryo dunes.

3 Over time, vegetation, such as marram grass, helps to establish and stabilise sand dunes, creating foredunes.

4 As the vegetation around the foredunes decomposes, nutrients are released into the sand. This allows a wider range of plants to colonise the dunes.

Formation of beaches

Beaches form from the deposition of material by waves.
- Low-energy constructive waves create **sandy beaches**.
- High-energy constructive waves create **shingle (pebble) beaches**.

You may find it useful to label each step with a number.

 Worked example **Grades 5–7**

Describe the processes involved in the formation of sand dunes. **[6 marks]**

1. Prevailing onshore winds transport sand towards the back of sandy beaches forming sand dunes.

2. Sand deposits where there is an obstruction, such as rocks, blocking the wind. This process continues, and sand builds up around the obstruction, forming a small embryo dune.

3. Over time, the dunes are colonised by pioneer species of plant, which strengthens and stabilises them. The plants trap more sand, increasing the size of the dunes and forming foredunes.

4. Decomposing plants release nutrients, allowing new plant species to colonise the dune. This process continues, and the dunes grow larger and more established. New embryo dunes begin to form in front of them.

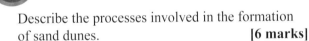

 Exam-style practice **Grades 2–7**

1 Describe the processes involved in the formation of a spit. **[6 marks]**

2 State the wave type that creates sandy beaches. **[1 marks]**

 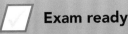

Hard engineering

The impact on coastlines of natural processes, such as erosion and longshore drift, has to be carefully managed to protect the environment and allow humans to live and work safely in coastal areas. Hard engineering strategies involve management through the use of man-made structures, each with advantages and disadvantages.

 Hard engineering strategies

Sea walls

Sea walls are concrete structures that are usually curved. They are designed to **reflect** wave energy.

👍 They can provide a promenade.

👍 They reduce erosion and flooding.

👎 They are very expensive to install and maintain.

👎 They are visually obtrusive.

Groynes

Groynes are barriers that stretch out into the sea at right angles. They reduce the effects of longshore drift by preventing sand from being washed away.

👍 They are relatively cheap.

👍 They retain sediment to maintain the beach.

👎 They are unattractive.

👎 They reduce space for recreational activities.

👎 They can deprive beaches of material further along the coast as they trap sediment.

Rock armour

Rock armour, or riprap, is composed of large boulders that **absorb** wave energy.

👍 It is relatively cheap.

👍 It is quick to implement.

👎 It is unattractive.

👎 It can become damaged during heavy storms.

Gabions

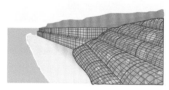

Gabions are wired cages of rocks that **absorb** wave energy. They are only used on sandy beaches.

👍 They are relatively cheap.

👍 Over time, they will be covered by vegetation.

👎 They have a short lifespan as they can rust and break.

👎 They are unattractive.

 Worked example   Grade 6

Suggest how sea defences, such sea walls, can help protect the coastline. **[4 marks]**

Sea walls, such as the one at Porthleven in Cornwall, form a physical barrier between the coastline and the waves, protecting the coastline from erosion. Sea walls also effectively protect the coastline from erosion because they are made of concrete and are often curved, which helps them to reflect wave energy. This limits erosion of the coastline.

Exam-style practice   Grades 4–6

Figure 1 Sea defences in Scarborough, Yorkshire

(a) Give the name of **one** sea defence shown in **Figure 1**. **[1 mark]**

(b) Describe **one** advantage and **one** disadvantage of using this particular sea defence. **[4 marks]**

 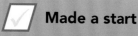

Soft engineering

You need to know the advantages and disadvantages of various soft engineering strategies, such as beach nourishment. These are strategies that use the existing local environment rather than adding artificial structures.

10 Soft engineering strategies

Beach reprofiling
Beach reprofiling involves the mechanical transfer of sand and shingle to change the shape of the beach so that it absorbs more wave energy. The material is usually transferred from the lower to the upper beach.

👍 It enhances natural recovery of dune face erosion.

👍 It protects buildings on the seafront.

👎 It is only a short-term solution.

👎 It can be expensive.

Beach nourishment
Beach nourishment involves depositing sand or shingle onto an eroded beach, replacing that which has been washed away, to widen it.

👍 It increases tourism potential.

👍 It protects buildings on the seafront.

👎 It requires constant replenishing.

👎 It can be expensive.

Dune regeneration
Sand dunes absorb water and wave energy. Sand dune regeneration involves the artificial creation of new dunes or the restoration of existing dunes. Adding plants, such as marram grass, to a dune can stabilise it, while building boardwalks and fences can offer protection to dunes.

👍 It helps to maintain a diverse natural environment that supports wildlife.

👍 It protects buildings on the seafront.

👎 Dunes can be easily damaged by storms.

In the short term, soft engineering options are often less expensive than hard engineering options. However, they usually need replacing more frequently, so over time they can be expensive.

5 Managed retreat

Managed retreat means allowing designated areas of the coast that are considered to be of low value to flood. It often involves the removal of current defences.

👍 It is a sustainable approach that doesn't interfere with natural processes.

👍 It results in salt marsh habitats that are rich in plant and marine life.

👎 It is a comparatively cheap management option, although it may be necessary to compensate people for loss of buildings or farmland.

👎 It is not always popular with locals.

👎 Saltwater can have a negative impact on existing ecosystems.

Named example
Northey Island in Essex was one of the first managed retreat schemes in the UK.

5 Worked example — Grade 5

Figure 1 A beach reprofiling project

Look at **Figure 1**. Give **one** advantage and **one** disadvantage of beach reprofiling as a coastal management strategy.

Advantage: It encourages the natural recovery of the surrounding dunes.

Disadvantage: It is only a short-term solution and will need repeating. **[2 marks]**

Another advantage of beach reprofiling is that it protects buildings on the seafront. Another disadvantage is that it can be expensive.

5 Exam-style practice — Grades 4–6

1 Suggest why a managed retreat policy might be adopted along a coastline. **[4 marks]**

2 Outline **one** way sand dune regeneration helps to protect the coastline. **[2 marks]**

Coastal management

You may be asked to give details about an example of coastal management that you have studied. This page uses Walton-on-the-Naze as the named example.

② Named example

Walton-on-the-Naze, Essex

Population: over 12,000

Main income: tourism

Attractions: Naze Tower, near-by nature reserves and it is a Site of Special Scientific Interest (SSSI) for its geology.

Key fact: on-going heavy erosion of the coastline threatens businesses and homes, as well as conservation efforts.

⑤ Coastal issues

The coastline at Walton-on-the-Naze is eroding quickly. The cliffs are regularly affected by slumping. The cliffs consist of London Clay and Red Crag, which are easily eroded by sea water. It is estimated that they are eroding at a rate of 2 metres per year. Longshore drift transports sand along the coast away from the beach. These issues affect the residents of the town, putting buildings and businesses at risk. Tourism is key to the local economy and sites of scientific interest and historic significance, such as the Naze Tower need protecting for both conservation and tourism.

⑩ Coastal management strategies and conflicts

A series of ongoing coastal management schemes have been introduced, including both hard and soft engineering strategies.

Hard engineering

In 1977, a series of hard engineering strategies were implemented to protect the coastline.

- A sea wall was built to prevent waves from hitting the cliffs and to protect the buildings nearest the sea.
- Drainage channels were also cut into the cliffs to allow water to run through them. This stops the cliffs from becoming saturated and limits further instability.
- Groynes were added to the beach to limit the effects of longshore drift by blocking the movement of sediment.

In 2011, the Crag Walk was installed as part of a heritage project; it uses rock armour to support a walk around part of the coastline.

Soft engineering

- In 1999, the beach was replenished with sand and gravel from nearby Harwich Harbour.

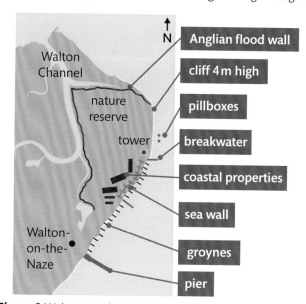

Figure 1 Walton-on-the-Naze

Social, economic and environmental issues

Hard engineering strategies cause an artificial change to the natural environment, which can conflict with some conservation strategies. Soft engineering strategies are relatively short term.

- The sea wall installation caused some damage to buildings. However, it has been highly successful in preventing further damage and needs little maintenance.
- Groynes have a short life of about 20 years, so they need restoring very regularly. However, they are relatively low cost.
- The crag walk has been expensive and has changed the coast significantly. However, it protects and preserves the conservation areas, as well as allowing tourists better access to the SSSI.
- The sand on the beach needed replenishing again by 2003.

Exam focus

Using specific details, describe why the management techniques were used. Then explain how well they worked and whether they had any negative impacts.

⑤ Exam-style practice Grade 5

Suggest how artificial changes to the coastal environment can affect conservation strategies.

[4 marks]

A river profile

As a river flows downstream from its source, the long and cross profile change due to the interaction of erosion, transportation and deposition processes. The long profile describes the gradient and the cross profile describes the cross-sectional shape of the river bed.

(15) River characteristics

Figure 1 The long and cross profiles of a river

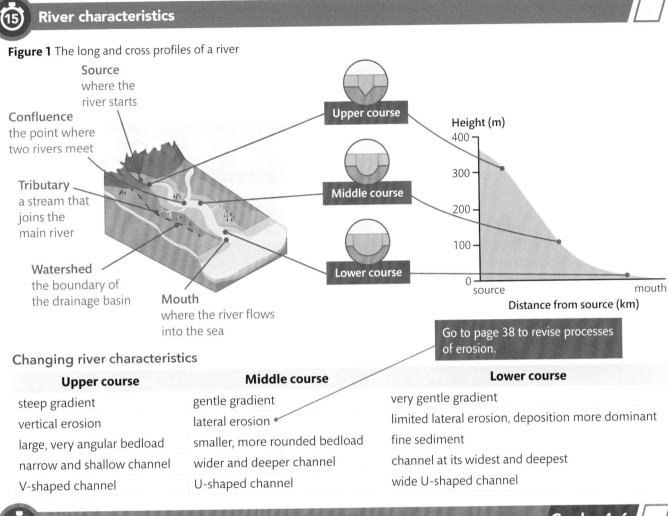

Source where the river starts

Confluence the point where two rivers meet

Tributary a stream that joins the main river

Watershed the boundary of the drainage basin

Mouth where the river flows into the sea

Upper course

Middle course

Lower course

Height (m)

Distance from source (km)

Go to page 38 to revise processes of erosion.

Changing river characteristics

Upper course	Middle course	Lower course
steep gradient	gentle gradient	very gentle gradient
vertical erosion	lateral erosion	limited lateral erosion, deposition more dominant
large, very angular bedload	smaller, more rounded bedload	fine sediment
narrow and shallow channel	wider and deeper channel	channel at its widest and deepest
V-shaped channel	U-shaped channel	wide U-shaped channel

(5) Worked example   Grades 4–6

Explain the reasons for the changes in the cross profile of a river as it flows downstream. **[4 marks]**

The source of a river is often on high land with steeper slopes. As the river flows over this land, it erodes vertically through hydraulic action, abrasion and attrition, leading to steep-sided V-shaped valleys and narrow, shallow river channels. The volume of water running through the channel (discharge) increases further downstream, partly due to the increased volume of water as tributaries join the river. This increased discharge, as well as increased velocity, leads to increased energy. Vertical erosion becomes less significant, and lateral erosion and deposition become more significant, creating wider and deeper channels and wider and flatter valleys. In the lower course of the river, the surrounding land is flat, the river's energy is low and deposition is more dominant than erosion.

(2) Exam-style practice   Grades 1–2

Which **one** of the following statements is the definition of a tributary? Shade **one** circle only. **[1 mark]**

A the point where a river flows out into the sea

B the point where a river begins

C a stream that joins the main river

 Made a start   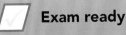 **Feeling confident**   **Exam ready**

Fluvial processes

Fluvial processes include erosion, which is the sculpting and wearing away of the landscape, and transportation, which is the movement of sediment within the river channel.

(10) Erosion

Types of erosion
There are two key types of erosion that occur at different stages of a river:
- **vertical** erosion (occurring downwards)
- **lateral** erosion (occurring sideways).

Processes of erosion
Hydraulic action – The force of the river hitting the banks and river bed can cause air to become trapped in cracks. The increasing pressure causes the banks to weaken and wear away.

Abrasion – Rock fragments carried by the river hit the banks and the bed, causing them to wear down.

Attrition – Rocks carried by the river collide with each other, which causes them to break and become smaller, rounder rocks.

Solution – Soluble rocks, such as limestone, dissolve in the river.

(10) Transportation and deposition

Transportation

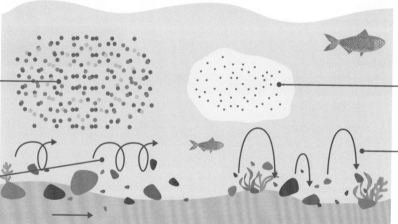

Suspension particles carried within the water

Traction the rolling of large pebbles along the river bed

Solution dissolved minerals carried within the water

Saltation the bouncing of small pebbles along the river bed

Figure 1 Transportation processes

Deposition
Deposition occurs when the energy of a river decreases and it no longer has enough energy to transport the material. This can happen where the river meets another body of water at the river mouth or where the water is shallower, such as on the inside of a bend.

(2) Worked example · Grades 1–2

Which **one** of the following statements describes the process of attrition? Shade **one** circle only.
[1 mark]

A the dissolving of rock types like limestone by a river ◯

B the action of rocks colliding into each other ◉

C the sheer force of water hitting the bed and banks of a channel ◯

Option A describes the process of solution and option C could describe the process of hydraulic action or abrasion, so option B is the correct answer.

(5) Exam-style practice · Grades 2–4

1 Give **one** process of river transportation.
[1 mark]

2 Explain how the combination of hydraulic action and abrasion causes change to the river channel.
[4 marks]

Made a start · Feeling confident · Exam ready

Fluvial erosion landforms

In the upper course of a river, vertical erosion from processes like hydraulic action is dominant. This leads to the formation of waterfalls, gorges and interlocking spurs.

⑩ Formation of waterfalls and gorges

 hard rock   soft rock

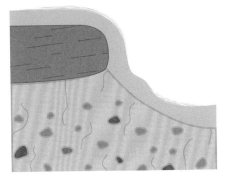

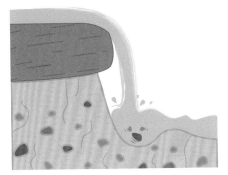

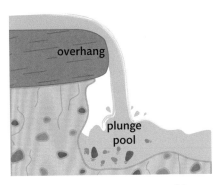

Waterfalls usually form in the upper course of a river where water flows over a band of hard rock that overlies a band of soft rock.

As the river flows over rapids, it forms a plunge pool. The erosion processes of hydraulic action and abrasion interact to undercut the soft rock and create an overhang.

Over time, the overhang is unable to support itself and it collapses under the force of gravity.

Figure 1 Waterfalls form where hard rock lies over soft rock.

The process shown in **Figure 1** repeats over centuries, causing the **waterfall** to retreat upstream and form a steep-sided valley, known as a **gorge**, such as Niagara gorge which is downstream from Niagara falls.

⑤ Interlocking spurs

Interlocking spurs form as the river flows around the areas of hard rock, finding the easiest route.

Named example

Figure 2 Interlocking spurs in Carding Mill Valley in the Shropshire Hills

⑩ Worked example   Grades 5–7

Explain the processes involved in the formation of a gorge.   **[6 marks]**

Gorges can be formed by erosion as a waterfall retreats up a valley. This happens when a river flows over a band of hard, resistant rock that lies over the top of softer, less resistant rock. The river erodes the softer rock faster, through the processes of hydraulic action and abrasion. This erosion leads to the undercutting of the softer rock. Over time, continued erosion causes an overhang of the hard rock to form. Eventually, the harder rock is unable to support itself and collapses, deepening the plunge pool, creating a steep drop between the top of the waterfall and the bottom. This process repeats, causing the waterfall to retreat upstream, leaving behind a steep and narrow gorge.

Describe the steps of the process and reference physical processes like hydraulic action.

② Exam-style practice   Grades 3–4

Describe **one** factor that can cause a gorge to form.   **[2 marks]**

Fluvial erosion and deposition landforms

Deposition occurs when the energy of a river decreases. When the river no longer has enough energy to transport sediment, it deposits it. The accumulation of this deposit results in the formation of a variety of different landforms.

 ## Deposition landforms

- A **levée** is an elevated bank along a river's edge. It forms when repeated flooding leads to deposition. The heaviest sediment is deposited first, as the river loses energy, and finer sediment (**alluvium**) is deposited further from the river.
- A **flood plain** is a wide, flat area of land on either side of a river that is often subject to flooding. Flood plains are composed of alluvium, left by deposition during floods.
- An **estuary** is a wide, sheltered body of water found at a river's mouth, where it broadens into the sea. It is a mixture of fresh water from the river and saltwater from the sea. As the river meets the sea at high tide, its flow slows, and sediment in the river and in the seawater is deposited. This deposited sediment forms **mudflats**. The mudflats are visible at low tide but are under water at high tide, and over time vegetation grows on them, forming salt marshes.

 ## Meanders

- **Meanders** are found in the middle to lower course of a river where the land is flatter.
- The combination of lateral erosion and deposition causes meanders to move and change shape.
- The line of fastest flow in the river causes erosion on the outside of the bend, creating a **river cliff**. Deposition occurs on the inside of the bend, where the flow is slower and the effect of friction is greater, causing a **slip-off slope** to form.

Named example

Figure 1 This meander on the River Severn consists of a sandy slope due to deposition and a river cliff due erosion.

 ## Ox-bow lakes

Erosion can cause both sides of a meander to migrate towards each other.

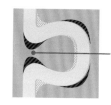

The neck becomes narrower and eventually the river breaks through.

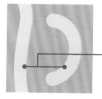

This forms a straighter channel and an ox-bow lake.

▨ areas of deposition ▨ areas of erosion

Figure 2 Ox-bow lakes form from meanders.

Worked example Grades 5–8

Explain the processes involved in the formation of ox-bow lakes. **[6 marks]**

Ox-bow lakes form as a result of lateral erosion, which causes both sides of a meander to migrate towards each other. This happens through processes like hydraulic action and abrasion. The erosion causes the neck of the meander to narrow over time until eventually, often during a flood, the river breaks through, creating a new, straighter channel. Over time, deposition causes the old meander to become cut off, creating an ox-bow lake.

Exam-style practice Grades 5–8

Study **Figure 1**. Explain the processes involved in the formation of meanders. **[6 marks]**

  Made a start **Feeling confident** **Exam ready**

Flood risk

A combination of physical and human factors increase the risk of flooding, which has social, economic and environmental effects.

(10) Factors affecting flooding

Factor	Increased flood risk	Decreased flood risk
land use (human)	Urban areas have more impermeable surfaces, such as concrete, which increases surface run-off and causes water to reach drains and the river faster. Some types of agriculture can leave the soil exposed, which also increases surface-run off.	Areas of vegetation, particularly forested areas, have a higher rate of infiltration – they absorb more water.
precipitation (physical)	Sustained periods of heavy precipitation result in the land being unable to absorb any more water and becoming saturated quickly.	Lighter, shorter and intermittent periods of precipitation allow the soil to absorb the water, reducing surface run-off.
relief (physical)	Areas with a steeper gradient (steeper slopes) encourage faster movement of water running across the land towards the river.	Areas with a smaller gradient (gentle slopes) cause water to move across the land much more slowly.
geology (physical)	Impermeable rocks, such as granite, do not allow water to infiltrate, increasing surface run-off.	Permeable rocks, such as limestone, allow water to infiltrate, which reduces the amount of surface run-off.

(2) Effects of flooding

Social
Effects on people can include:
- sustaining injuries (short-term)
- damage to property (short-term).

Economic
Effects on the wealth of the area can include:
- reduced tourism (long-term)
- cost of repairs and restoration (short-term).

Environmental
Effects on the surrounding landscape can include:
- destruction of crops (long-term)
- loss of livestock (long-term).

(2) Named example

Mytholmroyd, Yorkshire, was flooded in 2015 when the River Calder burst its banks after heavy rainfall. It caused significant damage to properties.

Figure 1 Mytholmroyd in Yorkshire during the 2015 floods

You can also use the named example on page 45.

(5) Worked example — Grade 5

Explain how urbanisation and agriculture increase the risk of flooding. **[4 marks]**

Urbanisation involves the construction of buildings and roads. These are often made of hard materials, such as concrete, and create more impermeable surfaces. This leads to increased surface run-off, causing water to reach the river channel faster, which increases the potential for a river to burst its banks.

Agriculture increases the risk of flooding due to the way in which farmers use the land. Exposed soil is less capable of absorbing water, especially during a storm, leading to increased surface run-off.

Give an outline of urbanisation and agriculture and how these can lead to an increase in the risk of flooding.

(10) Exam-style practice — Grade 5

1 Explain how **two** physical factors cause an increased risk of flooding.

[4 marks]

2 Study **Figure 1**. Describe the potential economic and social impacts of this flood.

[4 marks]

Flood hydrographs

Flood hydrographs help scientists predict flooding patterns by showing how varying levels of precipitation affect a river during a storm. Precipitation is moisture that falls to the ground, such as rain, snow, sleet or hail.

(15) Flood hydrographs

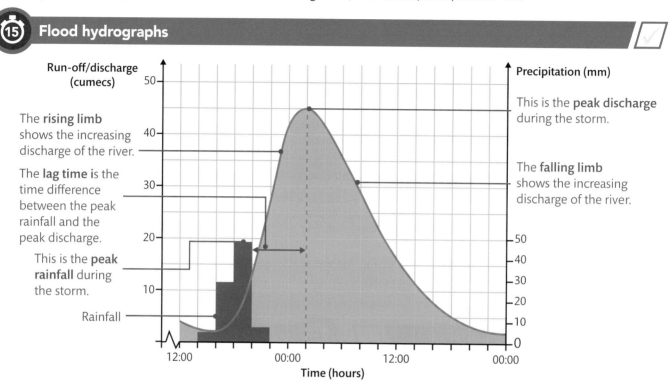

Run-off/discharge (cumecs)

The **rising limb** shows the increasing discharge of the river.

The **lag time** is the time difference between the peak rainfall and the peak discharge.

This is the **peak rainfall** during the storm.

Rainfall

Precipitation (mm)

This is the **peak discharge** during the storm.

The **falling limb** shows the increasing discharge of the river.

Time (hours)

Figure 1 A flood hydrograph is composed of a bar chart showing precipitation and a line graph showing the discharge of a river. The discharge of a river is the volume of water passing a particular point each second. It is measured in cumecs — cubic metres per second.

Factors affecting flood hydrographs

Hydrographs can be different shapes, depending upon the characteristics of a river and how likely it is to flood.

- A **flashy hydrograph** indicates that the river is more at risk of flooding. Flashy hydrographs have a steep rising limb, indicating the discharge of the river is increasing rapidly, and a short lag time, showing rainwater reaches the river quickly.
- A **gentle hydrograph** shows that a river is less at risk of flooding. Gentle hydrographs have a long lag time and a less steep rising limb, indicating that rain water is taking longer to reach the channel, so the river discharge is increasing slowly.

For factors affecting how quickly water reaches the river and increases the risk of flooding, see page 41.

(5) Worked example   Grades 4–6

Explain how geology can affect the shape of a flood hydrograph.   **[4 marks]**

If the land surrounding the river consists of lots of impermeable rocks, like granite, there will be less infiltration of water and therefore increased surface run-off. This causes the water to reach the river channel much faster, so the discharge increases more quickly, creating a flashy hydrograph. However, if the surrounding land consists of permeable rocks, water will infiltrate the rocks, increasing groundwater flow, so the rate at which the water reaches the channel is slower. This creates a gentle hydrograph.

When estimating the lag time, find the difference between the peak discharge and the peak rainfall.

Describe the appearance of the hydrograph for a small drainage basin and for a large drainage basin, giving reasons for the different shapes.

(10) Exam-style practice   Grades 3–5

1 Study **Figure 1**. Estimate the lag time.   **[1 mark]**

2 Explain how drainage basin size can affect the shape of a flood hydrograph.   **[4 marks]**

Hard engineering

You need to know about the advantages and disadvantages of various hard engineering strategies. Hard engineering strategies use physical structures to manage flooding.

 15 **Hard engineering strategies**

Dams and reservoirs

Figure 1 Drift Reservoir and its dam, Cornwall

A **dam** is a concrete barrier that restricts the flow of a river and creates an artificial lake known as a **reservoir**.

👍 Reservoirs can provide an additional source of water.

👍 They can be used as a source of hydroelectric power.

👍 They provide a source of drinking water.

👎 They're very expensive to install and maintain.

👎 They can cause farmland downstream to become less fertile as eroded material is deposited in the reservoir.

Embankments

Figure 3 Embankments are artificially raised river banks that allow a river to hold more water.

👍 They increase channel capacity, reducing potential flooding.

👍 They can be cheaper to install than other hard engineering strategies.

👎 They require regular maintenance.

👎 They can be eroded over time.

Straightening

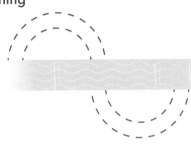

Figure 2 River channels can be artificially straightened by removing meanders. River channels can also be made wider and deeper.

👍 It allows water to flow faster, potentially reducing flooding.

👍 It can make the river easier and quicker to travel on for boats.

👎 It can cause flooding downstream due to the faster flowing channel.

👎 It can damage wildlife habitats as straightened banks can collapse.

Flood relief channels

Figure 4 Flood relief channels are artificial channels where water flows if the water levels are too high. The water is directed away to another area.

👍 They effectively reduce the risk of flooding in a particular location.

👍 They can provide opportunities for water sports.

👎 They can lead to flooding further downstream.

👎 They are extremely expensive.

---

5 **Worked example** **Grade 5**

Explain **one** advantage and **one** disadvantage of using embankments to manage rivers. **[4 marks]**

Embankments increase the amount of water a river can hold, which reduces the risk of flooding. However, they can be eroded over time by persistent rainfall.

5 **Exam-style practice** **Grade 5**

Study **Figure 1**. Explain **one** advantage and **one** disadvantage of using dams and reservoirs to manage rivers.

[4 marks]

Soft engineering

You need to know about the advantages and disadvantages of various soft engineering strategies. Soft engineering strategies use less invasive methods, working with the natural environment to manage flooding.

 Soft engineering strategies

River restoration

River restoration involves removing any hard engineering strategies and restoring a river back to its original course. This often involves making the river less straight, which slows its flow.

👍 Reintroducing meanders slows the river flow which reduces erosion.

👍 Unlike other strategies, there is no ongoing maintenance cost.

👎 Reintroducing meanders can make it more difficult to build near the river.

👎 In isolation, this approach doesn't usually reduce the risk of flooding significantly.

👎 It is not a guaranteed protection against flooding downstream.

Flood warnings and preparation

Flood warning systems provide people with advance information about possible floods.

👍 They reduce the impact of a flood.

👍 They give people time to move assets to a safer location, to position sandbags and to evacuate their homes.

👎 No action is taken to prevent the flooding itself.

👎 Some people may not receive the warning.

Flood plain zoning

Flood plain zoning policies control how land is used near or on flood plains.

👍 It reduces the risk of houses, schools and hospitals being flooded by limiting what is built.

👍 It can provide land for alternative uses, like pasture farming and parkland.

👎 It can decrease the value of land.

👎 The pressure for more housing can result in development projects being given authorisation to build on land which is susceptible to flooding.

> **Infiltration** is the movement of surface water into the soil. **Transpiration** is the process by which water moves through a plant.

Afforestation

Trees are planted near the river channel.

👍 It creates new wildlife habitats and can make an area more attractive.

👍 It increases infiltration and transpiration, reducing surface run-off.

👎 It takes time for trees to grow and mature to be effective.

👎 Afforestation alone doesn't prevent flooding.

🕐(5) **Worked example** **Grade 5** ✓

Suggest the possible benefits of using **two** hard engineering strategies and **two** soft engineering strategies in an urban area vulnerable to flooding.
[4 marks]

A benefit of using hard engineering strategies such as a flood relief channel in an urban area is that it would give all the homes and businesses in the area a high level of protection from flooding. A benefit of straightening the channel would be to increase its capacity, making flooding in the area less likely to occur. A benefit of using flood warnings, a soft engineering strategy, is that there is likely to be a high population density in an urban area and it would allow people time to evacuate before a flood. A benefit of afforestation, another soft engineering strategy, is that it reduces surface run-off, which may be a problem in an urban area.

> You need to use information from this page and page 43 on hard engineering.

> Relate your answer directly to the strategies of an urban area. Understanding the advantages and disadvantages of each river management strategy will make it easier to choose the most appropriate strategies.

🕐(2) **Exam-style practice** **Grades 1–2**

Which **one** of the following statements describes a disadvantage of using river restoration to manage flooding? Shade **one** circle only.

[1 mark]

A It doesn't prevent flooding. ◯

B It may decrease the value of land. ◯

C Restoring the river to its natural course is not a guaranteed protection against flooding downstream. ◯

Flood management

You may be asked to give details about an example of flood management that you have studied. This page uses Boscastle.

⑤ Named example

The Boscastle flooding, 2004

> You can also use this as an example of extreme weather in the UK.

Figure 1 Flooding at the Wellington Hotel, Boscastle, in 2004

Location: north Cornwall

Local rivers: Boscastle is at the confluence (where tributaries meet) of three rivers – Valency, Jordan, and Paradise.

Cause of flooding: exceptionally high level of rainfall. Over 60 mm of rainfall (typically a month's rainfall) fell in two hours, making the River Valency flood the town. The ground was already saturated following two weeks of heavy rainfall and the flooding coincided with a high tide, worsening its impact.

Damage: 58 properties were seriously damaged; over 100 cars were swept away; residents were trapped and forced onto roofs to escape the water.

⑩ Worked example — Grades 5–7

Using an example you have studied, describe the environmental and economic issues associated with **one** flood management scheme. **[6 marks]**

The flood management scheme at Boscastle cost a total of £10 million to implement. It included raising a car park so that it was above the flood level, which would reduce the financial loss from damage to vehicles if there was a flood in future. The scheme also led to the removal of trees near the banks of the river, which may have had a negative impact on wildlife habitats. However, in the flood plain above Boscastle, trees were cut back, which will allow a greater variety of plant species to flourish and encourage wildlife…

Exam focus

This is only part of a student's answer, but it shows how to structure a response to the extended writing questions. Make points about both environmental and economic issues and then support your points with specific details from your named example.

⑩ Flood management scheme

The Boscastle flooding endangered many lives, properties and businesses, and seriously affected the local environment. After the 2004 flooding, new flood management strategies were put in place to reduce the risk of any future floods.

Hard engineering strategies in Boscastle

- The river channel was artificially widened and deepened so that it could accommodate more water.
- The River Jordan drainage culvert was created to enable water to move more efficiently to prevent it backing up.
- New drains were installed to allow water to run into the lower section of the river quickly.
- The new car park built on the floodplain was raised above flood level to prevent vehicles being washed away during any future floods. It was also designed with a permeable surface to minimise damage to the structure.

Soft engineering strategies in Boscastle

- Trees near the river banks were removed as a precautionary step to minimise the risk of broken branches washing down stream and blocking the river channel or becoming a danger.
- The new car park was built next to the river because cars can be moved and the area left empty, which would lessen the impact of a flood. This is an example of flood plain zoning.

Issues

You need to know about the social, environmental and economic issues associated with your case study.

- **Economic issues** – Flood management schemes can be expensive. The Boscastle flood management strategies cost £10 million to implement.
- **Social issues** – Flood management strategies affect some people more than others. For example, in Boscastle, the widening of the river channel caused people to lose land and properties near the river.
- **Environmental issues** – Both soft and hard engineering strategies can have a negative impact on the environment. The tree management scheme in Boscastle destroyed some wildlife habitats.

> Issues can be positive as well as negative.

⑤ Exam-style practice — Grade 5

Explain **two** reasons for the installation of a flood management scheme that you have studied.
[4 marks]

Glacial processes

The movement of glaciers leads to a combination of processes acting on the landscape, including erosion, weathering, transportation and deposition.

Freeze-thaw weathering

Freeze-thaw weathering occurs when water freezes in cracks in rocks. As the water freezes, it expands and exerts pressure on the rock, leading to cracks. The repeated process of freezing and thawing over time results in the production of angular rock fragments, known as **scree**.

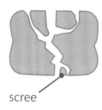

scree

Figure 1 Freeze-thaw weathering

Key processes

- ✓ **Plucking** – parts of the bedrock become attached to the base or sides of a glacier by freezing. As the glacier continues moving, these rocks are plucked out of the bedrock.
- ✓ **Abrasion** – over time, the bottom surface of a glacier becomes sharp and rough as a result of plucking and freeze-thaw weathering. Abrasion occurs when the bottom of a glacier rubs against bedrock and leaves behind a smooth surface with scratches, called **striations**.

Glacial movement

Transportation

- **Rotational slip** occurs when a glacier becomes lubricated from summer meltwater, which causes it to slide downhill. The glacier transports material within it.
- **Bulldozing** is the action of the **snout** (front) of a glacier pushing loose rock fragments forwards.

Deposition

Deposition occurs during melting or retreat. It takes place mainly at the snout of the glacier, where the greatest amount of ice melting occurs.

A retreating glacier causes rock fragments, known as **till**, to be left in an unsorted pattern, with rocks of different sizes and angularity.

Outwash is sand and gravel deposited by running water when the glacier melts. The material can be carried large distances before deposition in an outwash plain.

Ice in the UK

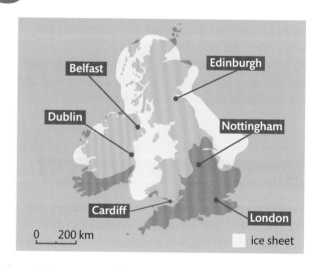

Figure 2 Ice coverage during the Devensian Period (the most recent glaciation), when ice stretched as far south as Cardiff

Worked example — Grades 1–2

Which **one** of the following statements describes the process of abrasion? Shade **one** circle only.

[1 mark]

A the action of a glacier rubbing rocks against a bedrock like sandpaper

B the action of a glacier removing loose fragments as it moves

C the action of water freezing in a rock, expanding and exerting pressure, leading to cracks

Exam focus

Make sure you know what all the glacial processes of erosion are. You should then be able to answer multiple choice questions like this quickly, giving you more time to spend on questions that require longer written answers.

Exam-style practice — Grade 4

❶ Describe **one** way glaciers transport material.
[2 marks]

❷ State the differences between plucking and abrasion.
[2 marks]

Glacial erosion landforms

Glacial erosion leads to the formation of distinctive landforms like corries, arêtes and pyramidal peaks. You need to know how these landforms are created.

 Glacial erosion landforms

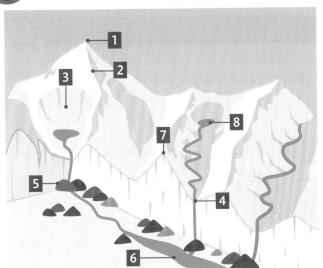

Figure 1 Glacial erosion landforms

① **Pyramidal peaks**, e.g. the Matterhorn, form when several corries and arêtes meet, and erosion leads to the formation of a single peak.

② An **arête**, e.g. Striding Edge in the Lake District, forms from erosion taking place on two back-to-back corries, forming a long, knife-edged ridge.

③ **Corrie**

④ **Hanging valleys** form when a small tributary glacier erodes more slowly than the main glacier. After the glaciated period, the valley formed by the tributary glacier is left hanging above the main valley. If there is a return of water, a waterfall is formed at the end of the smaller hanging valley.

⑤ A **glacial trough** forms when a glacier cuts through the original steep-sided, narrow V-shaped valley, and forms a wider U-shaped valley through the processes of abrasion and plucking.

⑥ **Ribbon lakes** form when a glacier flows over and erodes softer rock in glacial troughs. The glacier erodes softer rock to a greater depth than hard rock. Following the retreat of the glacier, meltwater collects in the deepened area, forming a ribbon lake.

⑦ **Truncated spurs** form when a glacier cuts straight through interlocking spurs.

⑧ **Tarn**

Geographical skills

Mention specific elements that you can see in the image that support your point. Always refer to the image as it appears in the caption, for instance 'Figure 2'.

 Corrie formation

A **corrie** forms from the accumulation of snow in a hollow. The size of the hollow is increased by snow becoming compacted under the weight of further snowfall and processes such as freeze-thaw weathering, eventually leading to the formation of glacial ice. Over time, plucking causes the back wall to steepen, and rotational slip and abrasion cause the hollow to deepen. At the front of the corrie, where erosion is at its lowest, materials are deposited and **moraine** (eroded material) builds up to form a raised lip. When the ice melts, it leaves a lake, known as a **tarn**.

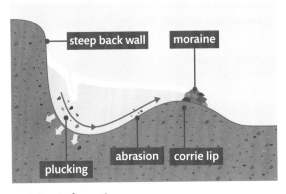

Figure 2 Corrie formation

 Worked example **Grades 5–7**

Study **Figure 2**. Explain how a combination of processes cause the formation of a corrie.

[6 marks]

A corrie forms from the initial accumulation of snow in a hollow on the side of a hill. Freeze-thaw weathering causes the hollow to increase in size, resulting in the gathering of more snow, as shown in Figure 2. During the glacial period, plucking causes the back wall to become steeper, and a combination of abrasion and rotational slip cause the hollow to deepen, indicated by the arrows in Figure 2 showing the direction of erosion. A raised lip is formed from the build-up of moraine, as labelled on the right of Figure 2, at the front of the corrie where deposition is dominant.

 Exam-style practice **Grades 4–5**

① Describe how arêtes are formed. **[2 marks]**

② Explain how erosion processes lead to the formation of glacial troughs. **[3 marks]**

 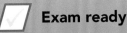

Glacial transportation and deposition landforms

The combination of transportation and deposition leads to the formation of drumlins, erratics, and different types of moraine. You need to know how these are formed.

⏱ Moraine

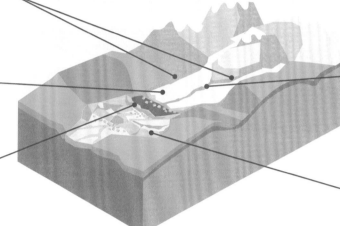

Lateral moraine
Material gathers at the edge of the glacier due to freeze-thaw weathering.

Ground moraine
Other material deposited by the glacier. They are disorganised piles of rocks.

Recessional moraine
A series of ridges form from the gathering of material behind the terminal moraine.

Medial moraine
Material gathers down the middle of the glacier.

Terminal moraine
Material gathers and forms a high ridge at the snout of the glacier.

Figure 1 Types of moraine

⏱ Drumlins

Drumlins are egg-shaped, raised areas of land formed from moraine, found in clusters along a glacial trough: the steeper, blunt end faces the direction the ice is coming from, and the smoother, tapered end faces away. Their long axis helps us to know the direction the glacier moved in.

Named example

Figure 2 Drumlins in the Lake District National Park

⏱ Erratics

Erratics are large boulders that appear out of place compared with their surroundings, left behind after being transported and deposited by a glacier.

Named example

Figure 3 Erratic boulders in Snowdonia National Park

⏱ Exam-style practice   Grade 4

Explain how scientists can determine the direction of glacier movement from the shape of drumlins.   **[3 marks]**

✓ **Made a start**   ✓ **Feeling confident**   ✓ **Exam ready**

Economic activities

Glaciated upland landscapes provide ideal spaces for economic activities like farming, tourism, forestry and quarrying. You need to know about the conflicts that exist between these different uses of the land and between development and conservation.

Tourism

People come to see the spectacular views that are typical of glaciated landscapes. They also take part in activities like walking, climbing, biking and winter sports.

👍 Tourism can boost the economy of the local area.

👍 This creates jobs and brings customers to local businesses.

However, large numbers of tourists can negatively impact conservation and development in these areas.

👎 Visiting tourists can have a negative impact on the conservation of glaciated landscapes. They may drop litter, disrupt ground-nesting birds and cause paths to erode.

👎 Tourism can lead to pressures to develop an area, as tourists may want facilities such as visitor centres and hotels. However, this is in conflict with conservation principles; many glaciated upland areas are protected by law, particularly national parks, which makes it very difficult to get planning permission.

Farming

Glaciated upland landscapes are traditional locations for sheep farming because many breeds of sheep are well-adapted to the thin infertile soils, steep slopes and short growing season. Arable farming, such as the growing of cereal crops or potatoes, is more suited to lowland valleys where the soil is more fertile.

👎 This means that it can be difficult for farmers to make a profitable living. It has led some farmers in glaciated upland landscapes to diversify by setting land aside for campsites or converting farm buildings into holiday rentals.

👍 This can add to a farmer's income.

👍 It can attract more visitors to the area.

👎 Land used for farming and campsites cannot be conserved as a wilderness area, and it may have a negative impact on wildlife.

Quarrying

The hard, resistant rocks that make up glaciated upland landscapes are ideal for quarrying to provide materials for the construction of roads and buildings.

👍 The development of quarries can provide employment opportunities.

👎 Quarrying can cause heated protests by environmental campaigners, as the pollution and disturbance it causes can harm the environment.

Forestry

UK glaciated upland landscapes provide ideal conditions for the growth of conifer trees, a source of timber.

👍 Developing conifer plantations contributes to the economy of an area, as it creates jobs.

👎 It can negatively impact conserving the natural habitats of upland areas, as native species of tree may be felled in order to clear land for commercial conifer plantations.

Land use conflicts

✓ Conifer plantations may have a negative impact on tourism, as they can obscure views.

✓ Tourism can cause conflicts with farmers, as visitors may damage crops or leave gates open.

✓ Quarrying can cause conflicts with locals as it is noisy and can lead to traffic congestion.

✓ Tourists can cause conflict with local people, as large number of holiday properties and second homes may inflate house prices, making it difficult for local people to afford to live in the area.

Worked example   Grade 3

Give **two** reasons why the development of a quarry in a glaciated upland landscape may cause conflict.
[2 marks]

The land surrounding the quarry development can no longer be used for outdoor recreational activities such as walking, cycling and horse riding. Quarrying also creates large volumes of dust, which may have a negative impact on the health of people living nearby.

Exam-style practice   Grade 4

Suggest how farming and forestry can provide opportunities in glaciated upland landscapes.

[4 marks]

Tourism in Snowdonia

You may be asked to give details about an example of tourism in a glacial landscape that you have studied. This page uses Snowdonia as the named example.

② Named example

Snowdonia National Park

Location: north Wales

Income: tourism (over 4 million visitors each year)

Attractions: Mount Snowdon (350,000 visitors reach the peak each year); Harlech Castle (90,000 visitors each year); copper mines and adventure activities.

Key facts:

- It is the largest National Park in Wales.
- Mount Snowdon is the largest mountain in England and Wales.

Figure 1 Hikers at the summit of Mount Snowdon

⑤ Impacts of tourism

You need to know about social, economic and environmental impacts of tourism. While tourism within the National Park has brought opportunities, it has also led to conflicts with landowners and environmentalists.

Positive impacts of tourism	Negative impacts of tourism
The Snowdonia National Park provides employment to a significant proportion of the population (social impact).	Many of those employed are on seasonal contracts so only work during the peak tourist season (social and economic impact).
Tourism generates approximately £396 million for the local economy every year (economic impact).	Average house prices are rising due to the increased demand for holiday homes (economic impact).
Visiting Snowdonia may increase people's interest in, and desire to conserve, wild places and the habitats of the plants and animals that live there (environmental impact).	Footpath erosion, litter and unauthorised access through farmland have negatively affected the local environment and wildlife habitats (environmental impact).
Places of historical and cultural interest such as Harlech Castle have an educational value (social impact).	Traffic congestion during the summer months creates delays for locals (social impact).

⑩ Worked example　　Grades 5–7

Discuss the social and economic impacts of tourism on glaciated environments.　　**[6 marks]**

One social impact of tourism on glaciated landscapes is traffic congestion. Approximately 10.5 million visitors explore Snowdonia National Park every year, predominantly in cars. This increases the volume of traffic on the roads, particularly during the summer months. This congestion causes problems for the locals who are going about their daily lives…

Exam focus

This is only part of a student answer to this question. The student has made a clear point and developed it with specific detail. To achieve higher marks, you would need to include another well-developed point on the economic impacts along with specific and relevant facts.

② Tourism management strategies

1 Place fences around environmentally vulnerable areas to prevent tourists entering and build designated walkways so they keep away.

2 Use information boards to increase awareness of the importance of protecting the environment.

3 Encourage businesses to be more sustainable and reward them with funding and recognition.

⑩ Exam-style practice　　Grades 2–4

1 Describe **one** environmental impact of tourism on glaciated environments.　　**[2 marks]**

2 Explain how tourism can be sustainably managed in glaciated environments.　　**[4 marks]**

Made a start　　Feeling confident　　Exam ready

Levelled response questions

Paper 1 contains levelled response questions worth 6 marks, which may be accompanied by a resource such as a photo or a diagram.

 Key skills

- ☑ Provide detailed explanations that demonstrate your knowledge and understanding.
- ☑ Accurately use specialist terminology.
- ☑ Make full use of any additional resources provided. You must refer to resources specifically in your answer, using them to support the points you are making.
- ☑ Ensure your answer has a logical structure.

 Worked example Grades 5–8

Using **Figure 1**, explain the processes involved in the formation of the headland features shown.

[6 marks]

Coastal arches and stacks, like the ones shown in Figure 1, begin as lines of weakness in a headland, known as faults. Over time, these faults become wider and develop into sea caves as a result of erosion processes such as hydraulic power. Hydraulic power refers to the process where the force of the water repeatedly impacts upon the lines of weakness in the headland, causing them to break apart.

Continued erosion results in the backs of two caves meeting, causing an arch to form. Powerful destructive waves, as shown in Figure 1, undercut the bottom of the arch through erosion processes such as abrasion, where fragments of rock are hurled at the bottom of the arch, wearing it away. Also, mechanical weathering occurs on top of the arch, further weakening it until eventually it is unable to support itself and collapses. This leads to the formation of a column of rock, known as a stack.

The answer provides a clear sequence for the formation of features. It makes links between the interaction of erosion and weathering in the formation of the arch.

Figure 1 The Green Bridge in Wales

Make sure you include detailed explanations demonstrating your knowledge and understanding of the topic.

To achieve maximum marks in this question, you must specifically refer to **Figure 1**. This answer clearly explains how the powerful waves that are shown contribute to the formation of a stack.

 Exam-style practice Grades 5–8

Using **Figure 2**, and your own knowledge, explain how the landforms shown are created by transportation and deposition processes.

[6 marks]

Figure 2 Dawlish Warren in Devon

 Made a start 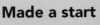 **Feeling confident** **Exam ready**

Urbanisation characteristics

Urbanisation is the increase in numbers of people living in urban areas compared to rural areas.

 ## Urbanisation patterns and trends

In 1950, two-thirds of the world's population lived in rural areas and one-third in urban areas. By 2050, this is likely to be reversed, with more than 6 billion people living in urban areas.

Urbanisation is happening faster in LICs and NEEs than in HICs because HICs are already extremely urbanised. There may also be problems like transport congestion and a lack of affordable housing in cities in HICs, which can lead to **counter-urbanisation**. Between now and 2050, 90 per cent of the expected increase in the world's urban population will take place in Africa and Asia.

Between them, India, China and Nigeria are expected to account for 37 per cent of the projected growth of the world's urban population by 2050. India is expected to add 404 million urban dwellers, China 292 million and Nigeria 212 million.

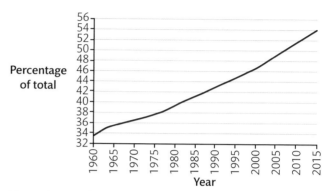

Figure 1 A graph showing the percentage of the global population living in urban areas, from 1960 to 2015

 ## Factors affecting the rate of urbanisation

Migration

Rural-urban migration (when people move from rural areas to urban areas) affects the rate of urbanisation. Reasons for migration can be categorised as either **push factors** or **pull factors**.

- Push factors are reasons that people leave a place, such as a lack of key services, poor transport links and low-paid employment.
- Pull factors are things that attract people to a place, such as good medical facilities, a range of entertainment options and higher-paid employment in the city.

Natural increase

Natural increase (when the birth rate is higher than the death rate) also affects the rate of urbanisation. It occurs when the birth rate is higher than the death rate in an area. This is more likely to occur in urban areas, where there tends to be a higher number of young adults of reproductive age, and better health care and standard of living.

 ## Characteristics of megacities

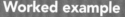 ## Worked example Grades 5–7

- ✓ A **megacity** is a city with over 10 million inhabitants.
- ✓ Over the last 15–20 years, the number of megacities has increased rapidly.
- ✓ There are megacities in developed countries, such as Tokyo in Japan, with a population of over 35 million people.
- ✓ The majority of megacities are in Asia, where there are many countries with emerging economies and rapid rates of urbanisation – there are five megacities just in India.
- ✓ Between now and 2050, the majority of new megacities are likely to appear in LICs and NEEs.

Explain the factors that affect the rate of urbanisation. **[4 marks]**

One of the main factors that affect the rate of urbanisation is rural-urban migration. People living in rural areas will often choose to move to urban areas, influenced by push and pull factors. For example, in the countryside farming is the main source of income, which is low paid. Many people move to the cities in search of higher-paid employment. Another factor affecting the rate of urbanisation is natural increase, which is when the birth rate is higher than the death rate, as natural increase tends to be higher in urban areas.

Exam-style practice Grades 2–3

Give **one** push and **one** pull factor affecting urbanisation.

[2 marks]

Expanding Mumbai: opportunities

You may need to answer a question about urban growth in an LIC or NEE using a case study that you have studied. This case study looks at the causes of growth in Mumbai in India (an NEE) and the opportunities it has created.

⑤ Case study

The location and importance of Mumbai

Figure 1 Mumbai has good transport links to the rest of the country through its numerous rail and road networks.

- Mumbai is one of the most densely populated cities in the world.
- Mumbai contributes more than $300 billion to India's **gross domestic product** (**GDP**) and is responsible for 25 per cent of India's industrial output and 70 per cent of its maritime trade.
- It has a range of industries, from textiles to petrochemicals, and serves as the headquarters for many companies, including the Reserve Bank of India. The Taloja industrial area is a hub for major industries such as chemical and pharmaceutical production.
- It is the base for the Bollywood film industry, which released over 100 films in 2016.
- It stimulates economic development across the region, with a busy port system and large stock exchanges.

⑤ Population growth

Natural increase
Natural increase is a major cause of population growth in Mumbai. Housing conditions and healthcare provision in the city have improved, which means people are living longer. Additionally, the majority of migrants are young adults, who are more likely to have children, contributing to population expansion in Mumbai.

Migration
Push and pull factors have increased immigration:

- a reduced need for farm workers in rural areas due to the use of technology and more efficient farming techniques, known as the 'Green Revolution' (push factor)
- a lack of education and healthcare in rural areas (push factor)
- low-paid farming work with limited prospects for the younger generation (push factor)
- greater job prospects in the city with a wider range of higher-paid employment in sectors like textiles (pull factor)
- greater prospect of improved housing conditions with water and electricity (pull factor)

⑤ Economic and social opportunities

Economic opportunities
- An expanding population has created a demand for more goods and services, which creates employment opportunities. The city's growth has enabled many migrants to find jobs in the service sector, for example as couriers, cleaners and hairdressers.
- Small businesses thrive in the Dharavi slum, generating more than $650 million every year.

Social opportunities
- Healthcare access is improving: Sion Hospital, Mumbai's biggest public medical centre, has grown from providing 50 beds in 1950 to 1400 beds in 2015.
- There are more than 1000 primary and secondary schools in Mumbai, which provide greater opportunities for more children.
- In 2015, the Brihanmumbai Municipal Corporation were looking to increase access to safe water in the city.
- In 2016, an Indian utility company agreed a deal with the US Agency for International Development to work towards establishing legal and safe electrical connections to the slums of Mumbai.

② Exam-style practice — Grades 2–4

Using a city in an LIC or NEE you have studied, suggest **two** pull factors that have contributed to urban growth.

[2 marks]

Expanding Mumbai: challenges

You may need to answer a question about urban growth in an LIC or NEE using a case study that you have studied. This case study looks at the challenges of urban growth in Mumbai, India (an NEE).

 ## Challenges caused by rapid growth

Providing clean water, sanitation systems and energy
Access to clean water is limited, with the use of standpipes restricted to two hours in the morning in some areas. Around 60 per cent of households are connected to the city's sewerage system, so there are many open sewers and polluted streams that pose a health risk.
There is limited access to energy resources, with supply not meeting the needs of the population.

Slums and squatter settlements
The main form of housing is chawls. Built over 100 hundred years ago, chawls are overcrowded blocks of small one-room residences that are in danger of collapsing. Squatter settlements have grown rapidly, expanding onto private land. They tend to be poorly constructed and overcrowded.

Challenges of rapid urban growth in Mumbai

Managing enviromental issues
Millions of tonnes of waste are dumped into the Mithi River. Dwellers in the Dharavi slum work daily to recycle waste.
There are over 2 million cars in the city causing gridlocked roads and increasing air pollution. The government is introducing a monorail to reduce the number of cars being used.

Health and education
Rapid population growth has resulted in increased pressure on the already strained health and education services available. Despite the growth of the Sion Hospital in Dharavi, many people still have to wait a long time to be treated.
Education is improving, but still many schools are overcrowded and there's a shortage of teachers.

Reducing unemployment and crime
There is a shortage of skilled engineers and technicians, and most people work in the 'informal sector', which often involves dangerous working conditions, no job security and poor pay.
To tackle crime associated with fake banknotes, drug problems and organised violent crime, the government has taken steps towards making Mumbai a cashless society (demonetisation).

 ## Named example

Urban planning in Mumbai

The Dharavi government is trying to improve the lives of its slum residents by:

- promising a free new 28 m² house for every resident who has lived there since 2000
- improving water supplies and the sanitation system.

In addition, the Hamara Foundation help young people living on the streets by improving their education opportunities and reducing health risks.

Figure 1 A child in a slum collecting and sorting plastic bottles for recycling

 ## Worked example   Grades 1–2

Identify which statement correctly describes a push factor. Shade **one** circle only.   **[1 mark]**

A lack of education and healthcare

B family ties in the city

C greater job prospects

Exam focus

In order to achieve the higher marks in this question you will need to include specific facts from your case study to support your points.

 ## Exam-style practice   Grades 5–9

For a city in a low income country or newly emerging economy, evaluate the challenges created by rapid urban growth.   **[6 marks]**

    Made a start   **Feeling confident**   **Exam ready**

Distribution of UK population and cities

The UK's population is unevenly distributed. In 2014, more than 80 per cent of people in the UK were living in urban areas.

 UK population distribution

In 2016, the population of the UK was estimated to be 65.6 million people.

Factors affecting population density

Factors affecting population density can be categorised as physical or human. **Physical factors** that favour a higher population density include a temperate climate and low-lying, flat, fertile land. **Human factors** that favour a higher population density include availability of jobs, transport links and quality of services such as healthcare and education.

Population density in UK cities

The **highest population density** in the UK is in the south-east of England, particularly in and around London. The other areas of high population density are located around the UK's capital cities (Belfast, Cardiff and Edinburgh) as well as major cities like Birmingham, Liverpool and Manchester. The **lowest population density** is in the Scottish Highlands.

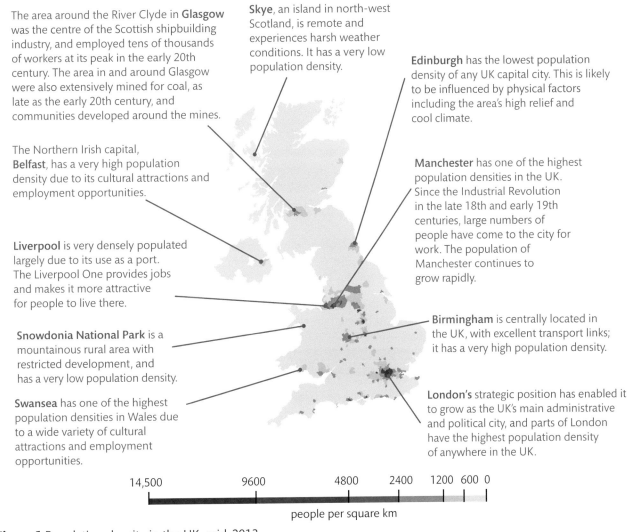

The area around the River Clyde in **Glasgow** was the centre of the Scottish shipbuilding industry, and employed tens of thousands of workers at its peak in the early 20th century. The area in and around Glasgow were also extensively mined for coal, as late as the early 20th century, and communities developed around the mines.

The Northern Irish capital, **Belfast**, has a very high population density due to its cultural attractions and employment opportunities.

Liverpool is very densely populated largely due to its use as a port. The Liverpool One provides jobs and makes it more attractive for people to live there.

Snowdonia National Park is a mountainous rural area with restricted development, and has a very low population density.

Swansea has one of the highest population densities in Wales due to a wide variety of cultural attractions and employment opportunities.

Skye, an island in north-west Scotland, is remote and experiences harsh weather conditions. It has a very low population density.

Edinburgh has the lowest population density of any UK capital city. This is likely to be influenced by physical factors including the area's high relief and cool climate.

Manchester has one of the highest population densities in the UK. Since the Industrial Revolution in the late 18th and early 19th centuries, large numbers of people have come to the city for work. The population of Manchester continues to grow rapidly.

Birmingham is centrally located in the UK, with excellent transport links; it has a very high population density.

London's strategic position has enabled it to grow as the UK's main administrative and political city, and parts of London have the highest population density of anywhere in the UK.

14,500   9600   4800   2400   1200 600 0

people per square km

Figure 1 Population density in the UK, mid-2013

 Exam-style practice Grades 2–4

Study **Figure 1**. Describe the distribution of the UK's population. **[3 marks]**

Expanding London: opportunities

You may need to answer a question about a major city in the UK using a case study that you have studied. This case study looks at the urban growth in London and the opportunities it has created.

(2) Case study

The location and importance of London

London is the UK's most populous city, as well as one of the world's most economically influential cities, with a population of more than 8.6 million people in 2015. It is located in the south-east of the UK near to a number of large airports, such as Heathrow. It is in a central global location (physically and in terms of time zone), which is ideal for business people who travel regularly to the east and west.

(10) Opportunities in London

Business

- London generates 22 per cent of the UK's GDP, even though it accounts for only 12.5 per cent of the UK population.
- In 2013, it was estimated that houses in London's top 10 boroughs were worth more than those in Northern Ireland, Scotland and Wales combined.
- In 2015, London had over 200,000 start-up companies, and hosted 17 of the largest businesses in the world in 2016.
- London has the second best global air connections in the world after Dubai.
- London is one of the world's top business centres, attracting highly skilled workers from across the globe.

Social and economic

- The city has a huge variety of recreational opportunities, including West End theatre shows, countless shopping centres and restaurants, and world-class sporting events. All of these entertainment options create thousands of jobs.
- It is well connected with an **integrated transport system**, including the Underground, buses, Tramlink, Docklands Light Railway, London River Services and the London Overground.

Environmental

- London has an ambitious **urban greening programme**, which includes the aim of being the first 'National Park City'.
- London includes eight royal parks, 8 million trees, 30,000 allotments, 3 million gardens and two National Nature Reserves.
- 47 per cent of the city consists of green space.
- Other urban greening opportunities include nest boxes, rain gardens, green roofs, and river jetties used for bird roosts.

(10) The impacts of migration on London's growth and character

There is rapid population growth: one-third of 335,000 net migrants to Britain in 2015 went to London.

Migration is adding to the number of skilled workers competing for jobs. Between 2000 and 2011, european migrants have made a net contribution of £20 billion to UK public finances.

There is social and racial tension between some migrants and locals.

Impacts of migration

Population growth has led to housing shortages, which the government are struggling to address.

Increased migration is putting more pressure on London's schools, with a shortage of both primary and secondary school places.

London is one of the most culturally diverse cities in the UK, with 37 per cent of residents born abroad. Migrants have introduced different types of foods, entertainment and clothing.

(5) Exam-style practice   Grade 5

Using a case study city you have studied, outline **two** ways its location creates opportunities.   **[4 marks]**

Made a start   Feeling confident   Exam ready

Expanding London: challenges

You may need to answer a question about a major city in the UK using a case study that you have studied. This case study looks at the urban growth in London and the challenges it has created.

⏱15 Challenges of urban growth

Housing

- Rising housing costs reduce living standards as a larger proportion of income is used on housing.
- The gap between the richest and the poorest has increased; those who already own property see it rise considerably in value, but it is becoming more difficult for other people to buy their first property.

Education

- By 2031, it is predicted that London will have 300,000 more 4–15 year olds than it does today. The city is already struggling to provide enough school places.

Healthcare

- Inconsistencies in the quality of healthcare within London have lead to some hospitals having long waiting lists.

Job opportunities

- London's unemployment rate has fallen in recent years, reaching 5.8 per cent January–March 2016, but it is still higher than the UK average, which was 5.1 per cent for the same period.

Inequality

- Urban deprivation: an independent study in 2015 found that, after considering housing costs, 27 per cent of Londoners live in poverty compared with 20 per cent for the rest of England.
- The poorest places tend to be in the eastern boroughs; but, recently, deprivation levels have been rising in the outer boroughs as affordable housing in inner London becomes harder to find.

Environmental

- The average household recycling rate for the city in 2016 was 32 per cent, which was the lowest in England.
- Many buildings became **derelict** following deindustrialisation, especially in East London.
- Development of **brownfield sites** can be expensive because old buildings have to be demolished, and land cleared.
- Urban sprawl is putting increasing pressure on London's **rural-urban fringe**. In March 2015, a report found that over 86,000 new houses were planned for greenbelt land around London.
- Increasing London house prices have contributed towards the rise in the number of commuter settlements around London, especially in Hertfordshire and Kent. Here house prices are also rising quickly, but they remain more affordable than London.

⏱5 Named example

Lower Lea Valley Redevelopment Project

You need to know the main features of a urban redevelopment project and why it was needed.

The Lower Lea Valley, a deprived part of East London, was selected as the key location for the Olympic Park. There were high rates of unemployment, a poor public health record and derelict industrial buildings.

- 👍 The 500-acre Olympic Park employed people both before and after construction.
- 👍 80 per cent of soil contaminated with industrial waste was washed and reused.
- 👍 The urban wasteland of the Lower Lea Valley was cleaned and 9000 new homes were built.
- 👍 Accessibility was increased through new land bridges built across rivers, roads and railways.

⏱2 Worked example — Grades 4–6

Explain how urban sprawl affects commuter settlements and the rural-urban fringe. **[4 marks]**

The rural-urban fringe is an area of mixed land uses, such as space for retail parks, farmland and golf courses. Urban sprawl increases competition for land in the rural-urban fringe, as new housing developments push up house and land prices in the areas around large cities. This can result in green spaces, such as agricultural land and large gardens in the rural-urban fringe, being sold off for houses to be built on them.

As major cities grow, house and land prices tend to increase, which can lead to an increase in the number of commuter settlements. These are towns and villages situated near major cities, where a large proportion of the population commute into the city for work. House prices often remain more affordable in commuter settlements than in the city. As a city expands, new commuter settlements may form...

⏱5 Exam-style practice — Grades 4–6

For an urban regeneration project you have studied, explain the reasons why the area needed regeneration.
[4 marks]

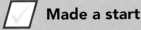 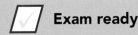

Urban sustainability

Sustainable urban living involves managing resources, such as energy, to meet today's needs whilst protecting the needs of future generations and the environment.

(5) Creating green space

Figure 1 'Gardens by the Bay' in Singapore is a sustainable green space in an urban area. It is home to 18 'supertrees', 11 of which have sustainable functions, such as harvesting solar energy for lighting.

Green spaces are areas partly or entirely covered by grass, trees or other vegetation. There are many benefits of green spaces in urban environments.

- Green spaces are characterised by their recreational and aesthetic appeal. They have a positive impact on people's mental and physical health.
- They are ideal habitats for wildlife and plants.
- They provide suitable environments for urban food production.
- Carbon emissions are reduced because plants absorb carbon dioxide during photosynthesis.

(5) Waste recycling

Recycling and reusing materials conserves natural resources and reduces waste production. In turn, this conserves energy and reduces pollution.

Sweden has one of the best household **waste recycling** systems in the world, with only 1 per cent of household waste ending up in a rubbish dump. Recycling stations are situated no more than 300 metres from any residential area, allowing Swedes to separate all recyclable waste in their homes and deposit it in special containers in their block of flats or drop it off at a recycling station.

In 2015, nearly 2.3 million tonnes of household waste was burnt and converted into energy. The 32 incineration plants produce heat for 810,000 households and electricity for 250,000 private houses.

(5) Conserving energy and water

Sustainable urban living involves conserving two resources which are essential for human life: energy and water.

- Cities can conserve water by recycling water used for washing and drinking for use in energy production.
- Singapore is a **water-stressed city**, which means that demand for water exceeds supply. It has made its water use sustainable by desalination, reclaiming water from sewers and treating it so it is safe to drink, and by efficiently catching and storing rainwater.
- Cities can conserve energy by renovating old buildings to improve their energy efficiency, installing solar panels to generate electricity, and by including high levels of insulation in new housing developments to reduce the amount of energy needed to heat them.

(5) Worked example — Grade 4

Explain how **one** urban transport strategy has been used to reduce traffic congestion. **[3 marks]**

Stockholm's peak time congestion charge is an example of an urban transport strategy that has helped to reduce congestion. Road users are charged for entering certain parts of the city between 06.30 and 18.30, which has contributed to a 22 per cent reduction in the number of vehicles entering the city centre.

Other suitable answers include:

- Hangzhou's public cycling system is one of the world's largest bike-sharing systems, with over 80,000 bikes and several thousand service points to date. This has helped to reduce the volume of traffic in the Chinese city.
- Copenhagen has an online ticketing system for its bike share scheme, Bycyklen, which also has touchscreens integrated into the bikes. The system is hugely popular, with 50 per cent of commuters using the bikes. This has contributed to Copenhagen's goal of being carbon neutral by 2025.

(10) Exam-style practice — Grades 5–9

Assess the importance of managing resources and transport to create sustainable urban living.

[9 marks] [+ 3 SPaG marks]

Made a start / Feeling confident / Exam ready

Classifying development – economic measures

There are variations between the levels of economic development in different countries around the world. You need to know about different measures of economic development and their limitations.

 ## Economic development indicators

There are lots of different measures of development. One economic measure of development is gross domestic product (**GDP**). GDP is the value of all the goods and services produced within a country. Another economic measure of development is gross national income (**GNI**). GNI is the total income of a country, which is the GDP along with any income obtained from other countries.

GNI can also be used to calculate another economic measure of development, **GNI per capita**. This is calculated by dividing the country's GNI by the size of the country's population. It is designed to give a measure of the average income of people living in that country. GNI per capita is used by the World Bank to divide countries into categories that reflect their level of economic development. In 2013, the World Bank used these categories:

LIC – Low Income Country. A country with a GNI per capita of $1025 or less

HIC – High Income Country. A country with a GNI per capita of $12,476 or more

NEE – Newly Emerging Economy. A country which has begun to experience higher rates of economic development and investment, usually with higher levels of industrialisation, and that no longer relies mainly on agriculture. Examples include India, China and Brazil.

thousands (current US$)

<6.80

6.80–16.23

16.23–29.29

29.29–51.75

>51.75

Figure 1 Gross national income (GNI) per capita in different countries (2014)

 ## Limitations

Although economic measures of development are useful for comparing levels of wealth between countries, they have several significant limitations.

- They do not show what percentage of the population receives what percentage of a country's income, so do not show inequality of wealth within a country – a country with a high GNI per capita may have some very rich people and a significant proportion of the population living in poverty, but economic development measures don't show this.

- Some countries may not have up-to-date data, particularly if they are developing quickly, whilst the governments of other countries may not provide accurate data – this means that economic measures can be unreliable ways of comparing levels of development.

- They do not reflect the quality of life, which is important in determining a country's level of development.

Go to page 60 to revise social measures.

 ## Worked example   Grades 3–4

Give **one** advantage and **one** disadvantage of economic measures of development.   [2 marks]

An advantage of economic measures is that they reflect standard of living - the amount of money people have to live on - but a disadvantage is that they do not reflect quality of life.

Exam-style practice   Grades 2–4

1 Give a definition of a High Income Country (HIC).   [1 mark]

2 Study **Figure 1**. Describe the global pattern of HICs.   [3 marks]

 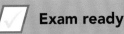

Classifying development – social measures

Development can also be compared using social measures, which show whether people in a country can expect to live a long and healthy life. Like economic measures of development, they have limitations if used separately.

(10) Social development indicators

There are other development indicators that geographers can use to assess a country's level of development, including:

1 **Birth and death rates** – the number of live births and the number of deaths, which are both measured per 1000 of the population per year. They provide an indication of a country's level of development. For example, a low birth rate may indicate a country has established a good education system, as higher levels of education contribute to more women choosing a career before, or instead of, having a family. A high death rate may indicate a lack of medical care or a country involved in conflict.

2 **Life expectancy** – the average lifespan of someone living in that country. Generally, more developed countries have a higher life expectancy. For example, in 2015, approximate life expectancy at birth was 82 in the UK and 59 in Uganda.

3 **Infant mortality** – this is the number of deaths of children under one year old and is measured per 1000 live births. This provides a reliable indication of a country's healthcare system.

4 **People per doctor** – this is measured per 1000 people and gives an indication of the healthcare system in place. In 2013, there were approximately 0.3 doctors per 1000 people in Afghanistan.

5 **Literacy rate** – this is measured as a percentage, and indicates the quality and accessiblity of a country's education system.

6 **Access to clean water** – this is measured as a percentage and indicates whether a country has established infrastructure in place, such as piped water to homes and water treatment plants.

Combining economic and social measures

The **Human Development Index (HDI)** was devised by the United Nations, and combines three measures of development: GNI per capita, life expectancy and number of years in education. This generates an average score from 0 to 1, with 1 being the highest.

(5) Advantages and limitations

- An advantage of the HDI as a measure of development is that it combines three different measures, one economic (GNI per capita) and two social, which gives a more comprehensive reflection of a country's development. In 2015, Norway had the highest HDI score, whilst the Central African Republic had the lowest.

- Like data provided for economic measures of development, data provided by the governments of some countries may not be accurate, or there may not be accurate data available for an entire country for a measure, meaning not all measures can be used to compare all countries. For example, data about death rates and life expectancy for a country involved in ongoing conflict may not be readily available, as it would be difficult to collect.

very high HDI score   very low HDI score

Figure 1 Map showing countries by their HDI score

(5) Worked example — Grade 4

Using **Figure 1**, compare the differences in HDI score between Africa and North America.

[2 marks]

The map indicates that the HDI values for the countries across North America are higher than those in Africa. Canada and the USA have very high HDI values, whereas in Africa some of the HDI values are much lower than North America.

Geographical skills

You need to be able to recognise and describe distributions and patterns of both human and physical features from a map.

(2) Exam-style practice — Grades 4–5

Suggest **one** limitation of using a social measure of development. **[2 marks]**

Made a start | Feeling confident | Exam ready

The Demographic Transition Model

The Demographic Transition Model (DTM) shows how a country's population changes over time in terms of their birth rates, death rates and total population size.

15 The Demographic Transition Model

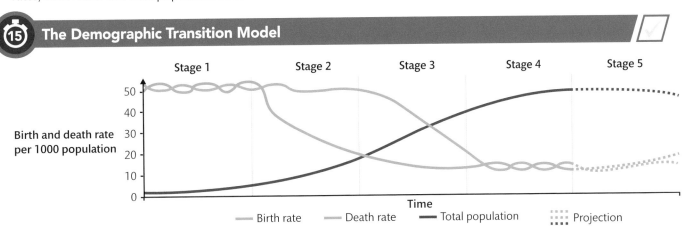

	Birth rate	Death rate	Population size	Example
Stage 1	High due to: • lack of birth control • tendency towards larger families because of cultural or religious beliefs • children working	High and fluctuating due to: • high infant mortality rate • disease and lack of healthcare • famine • lack of sanitation	Low	Amazon rainforest
Stage 2	Remains high	Starts to decline due to improvements in medical care and sanitation	Starts to increase	Bolivia
Stage 3	Declines rapidly due to: • increased availability of contraception • improved education • fewer children required to work for family's income	Continues to decline due to further medical developments and improvements to living conditions	Continues to increase	Mexico
Stage 4	Low and fluctuating	Low and fluctuating	High	UK or USA
Stage 5	Falls lower than death rates because desire for a large family decreases	Starts to increase slightly due to an ageing population	Starts to steadily decline	Japan

5 Worked example — Grade 5

Explain why birth rates are falling in stage 3 of the DTM. **[4 marks]**

In stage 3 of the DTM, birth rates fall due to changes in education and women's status, as many women choose to have a career before, or instead of, having a family. Alongside this, improved access to contraception and greater family planning awareness means people can choose whether they want to have a child.

Exam focus

For an 'explain' question you need to show in your answer that you understand why something happens. This example has two valid points and explains clearly how each affects the birth rate.

5 Exam-style practice — Grade 5

Outline **two** reasons why birth and death rates are high in stage 1 of the DTM. **[4 marks]**

Uneven development: causes and consequences

The global divide between rich and poor is growing, with half of the world's wealth owned by just 1 per cent of the population. You need to know the causes and consequences of uneven development.

 (10) Physical, economic and historical causes of uneven development

Extreme weather
Extreme weather hazards, such as tropical cyclones, may inhibit a country's ability to develop due to the frequent devastation caused and the cost of rebuilding. (physical)

Resources
Countries have different amounts of valuable natural resources such as oil, gas, gold and minerals. (physical)

Trade
World trade isn't equal, with many HICs and **transnational corporations (TNCs)** dominating the market. LICs tend to export low value raw materials to HICs, who manufacture more profitable goods. This means HICs get richer and LICs' development is limited. (economic)

Location
Landlocked countries may be unable to trade as easily, which affects economic growth. (physical)

Causes

Debt
Many LICs have high-interest debts with HICs so they can't spend money on developing. (physical)

Conflict
Countries involved in lengthy conflicts may be less developed, as resources have been used for war. High numbers of fatalities reduce the number of people of working age. (historical)

Colonialism
Colonialism – acquiring political control over another country and economically exploiting it – has led to the uneven development of some richer nations in comparison to the countries that they colonised. (historical)

 (5) Consequences

Disparities in wealth and health

Uneven development leads to huge disparities (differences) in wealth and health both within and between countries.

Since the financial crisis in 2008, wealth inequality has continued to rise. Approximately 70 per cent of the world's population owns wealth of less than $10,000, in comparison to 1 per cent owning over $1 million.

Uneven development also creates huge disparities in health. In 2016, a child born in Swaziland could expect to live for only 51–53 years, while a child born in Japan could expect to live for 81–89 years. Despite being one of the world's wealthiest countries, the USA has significant disparities in access to healthcare between the richest and poorest people in the population. This has resulted in notable differences in life expectancy within the country.

International migration

Uneven development has caused many people to leave their country of origin in search of a better quality of life, particularly better employment opportunities, and better healthcare and sanitation, which contribute to a higher life expectancy. Net migration to the UK has increased, with migrants seeking employment, which often pays more than a similar job would in their country of origin. Although migrant workers contribute to the UK's economy, immigration has put pressure on key services including education, health and housing.

 (5) Worked example **Grades 4–6**

Outline **two** economic causes of uneven development and their potential consequences for the health of a population. **[4 marks]**

Many LICs have high-interest debts with HICs, which can take a long time to pay back. This prevents the LICs from investing in things like, hospitals and emergency services, which could limit the amount of medical provision available to the population.

Transnational corporations (TNCs) also cause uneven development. TNCs are companies that operate in multiple countries. They typically originate in HICs. TNCs can contribute to uneven development by utilising cheap labour in less developed countries, and by imposing poor working conditions and long hours upon workers in LICs, which can harm their health.

International migration is caused by both push and pull factors (see page 52).

 (5) Exam-style practice **Grades 4–6**

Suggest how uneven development leads to international migration. **[4 marks]**

 Made a start **Feeling confident** **Exam ready**

Reducing the global development gap

There are various strategies that can be used to reduce the global development gap. You need to know an example of how the growth of tourism in an LIC or NEE helps to reduce the development gap. This page uses Brazil.

 Strategies to reduce the global development gap (15)

Fairtrade
Fairtrade ensures that farmers are consistently guaranteed a fair price for their crops, enabling them to improve their quality of life through a more stable income. Fairtrade schemes are not always successful, as certification imposes significant costs on poor growers.

Microfinance loans
Financial support, such as savings accounts, provided by small-scale banks help poor people set up their own business or improve their homes.

Intermediate technology
Simple technology that is easy to use and maintain for a range of economic activities enables locals to work self-sufficiently. It is often used in small-scale projects in LICs.

Debt relief
Writing off the the debt of heavily indebted poorer countries, enabling them to invest money in improving the population's quality of life.

Strategies to reduce the development gap

Investment
Money from TNCs or HICs can help LICs to improve infrastructure, such as roads and electricity supply, and increase employment opportunities.

Industrial development
Industrial development leads to increased employment, higher wages and improvements in housing and education. It has a **multiplier effect**, in which one change leads to more and greater changes.

Tourism
Visitors from HICs often spend a lot of money, which recipient countries can reinvest into improving infrastructure, housing, healthcare and education.

Aid
Useful resources donated by a country or NGO can come in different forms. Short-term aid, such as food and medical supplies, is usually provided in response to a natural disaster. Long-term aid, including training and materials, is social and economic development used to help a country become more self-sufficient.

 Worked example   Grades 2–4 (5)

1 How can microfinance loans help to reduce the development gap?   **[3 marks]**

Microfinance loans provide poor people with the money needed to operate and develop a small self-sufficient business. This enables them to improve their quality of life through being able to purchase clothes and food for their families.

2 Using an LIC or NEE that you have studied, outline **two** ways that tourism is helping to reduce the development gap.   **[3 marks]**

In Brazil, an NEE, tourism is helping to reduce the development gap by increasing employment opportunities; in 2014 tourism accounted for nearly 9 per cent of all employment. Tourism is also boosting Brazil's economy, generating income that has been invested in healthcare and education, which improves quality of life for the country's population.

 Named example (5)

Tourism in Brazil

- In 2016, Brazil attracted 6.6 million foreign tourists, contributing $6.2 billion to the economy. The number of tourists was boosted by the Olympic and Paralympic Games.

- Brazil receives the most foreign tourists of any South American country. The income from this has enabled further investment in education and healthcare to improve basic services.

- The increase in tourism has provided more employment opportunities: in 2014, direct and indirect employment in the travel and tourism sector in Brazil accounted for 8.8 per cent of all employment.

 Exam-style practice   Grades 2–3 (5)

Outline **one** way that intermediate technology helps to deal with the problems of unequal development.

[2 marks]

Emerging India: changes

You may need to answer a question about an NEE or LIC that is experiencing rapid economic growth using a case study you have studied. This case study looks at the economic development in India.

 Case study

India

India is the seventh largest country in terms of land mass. Its position in the middle of the *Indian Ocean* means that it has a wide range of ocean transport routes, which allows trade with other countries. It shares its international borders with six countries: Bangladesh, Myanmar, Bhutan, Nepal, Pakistan and China.

Politics

- As of 2017, India had a population of over 1.3 billion and is the second most populous country in the world.
- The country is a member of the World Trade Organization (WTO) and the UN.

Social

- In 2015, India had the largest diaspora (the spread of people from their country of origin) in the world, with over 16 million people from India living abroad.
- In 2015, life expectancy for women was 69.8 years and for men 66.9 years.

Culture

- India is a predominantly Hindu country, but it also has the third largest Muslim population in the world.
- The Indian film industry, which includes Bollywood, has the greatest number of admissions compared with other countries. The majority of these viewers are local, although Bollywood is expanding around the world. The Indian film industry produces approximately 1600 films each year.

Environment

- The country experiences two monsoon seasons: the north-east monsoon and the south-west monsoon, which occur at different times within the overall monsoon season of June–October.
- In 2014, India was ranked 155th out of 178 countries for its environmental quality.

Manufacturing and India's changing economy

- In recent years manufacturing industries – the secondary sector of the economy – in India have rapidly expanded. This has been encouraged by government initiatives such as Make in India, which is intended to make India a global manufacturing hub and create millions of jobs.
- The contribution of the secondary sector to India's economy has risen, whilst the contribution of the primary sector, particularly agriculture, has declined. This has led to increased rural–urban migration.
- The services sector, the tertiary sector, now makes the biggest contribution to India's GDP, which has resulted in a more skilled workforce and is reducing poverty.
- Parts of India's quaternary sector have grown rapidly, particularly the telecommunications network. Investments from TNCs have contributed to this change.

Trading relationships in India

India's top trading partner is China. It also has a strong political and trading relationship with the UK. Since the 1990s, changes to trading policies have seen a rapid rise in the quantity of India's imports and exports. Between 2006 and 2012, total merchandise trade in India increased from $252 billion to $794 billion.

In 2016, India's exports had a total value of approximately $261 billion. The second major export was mineral-related products, such as fuels and oils, which generated $27.7 billion. Export of pearls, precious stones, metals and coins generated over $43 billion in the same year.

Exam-style practice **Grade 4**

Using an NEE that you have studied, outline **one** way the secondary sector of the economy has changed. **[2 marks]**

  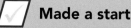 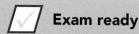

Emerging India: impacts

You may need to answer a question about an NEE or LIC that is experiencing rapid economic growth using a case study you have studied. This case study looks at the impacts of economic development in India.

(5) Rapid development

Increased volumes of traffic causes congestion and air pollution.

More job opportunities help to reduce the amount of poverty.

Better access to healthcare and education for some urban areas improves quality of life.

Impacts of rapid economic development

India has historically received aid from countries including the UK, Canada and the US, in the form of food, medical supplies and millions invested into projects to reduce poverty. It is becoming less dependent on international aid; in 2015, Britain stopped giving aid to India, and is now focusing on investment in trading relationships.

Difficulties providing sufficient housing for the growing population can lead to more squatter settlements.

Rising levels of water and air pollution, generated by the increasing population, can lead to health problems.

Food demand increases, which can present problems if supply is insufficient.

(5) Foreign investment

Since 1991, India has experienced increased investment from TNCs because of changes to government policy. Foreign direct investment was $233 million in 1992, but by 2015 it had increased to $44 billion.

Advantages
👍 improvements in infrastructure
👍 investment in health and education
👍 more job opportunities
👍 improved position in the global market

Disadvantages
👎 poor working conditions
👎 low pay
👎 environmental pollution

LAC stands for Latin America and Caribbean States.

To calculate a percentage increase, remember to subtract the original number from the new number and then divide the difference by the original number. Then multiply this by 100.

(5) Worked example   Grades 2–4

Study **Figure 1**.

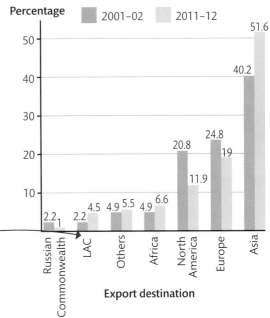

Figure 1 India's export destinations, 2001–02 and 2011–12

Calculate the percentage increase in India's exports to Asia.   **[1 mark]**

28 per cent

(10) Exam-style practice   Grades 5–9

'Rapid economic development leads to more problems than benefits.'
To what extent do you agree with this statement? Justify your decision.   **[9 marks]**

 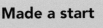

Causes of economic change

Over the past 50 years there have been major changes in the economy and the UK's employment structure. The primary and secondary sectors have declined, the tertiary sector has grown, and in recent years the quaternary sector has expanded rapidly.

(2) Four classifications of industry

1. **Primary** industries involve obtaining raw materials, e.g. mining, farming and fishing.
2. **Secondary** industries process raw materials into products, e.g. oil refining and food production.
3. **Tertiary** (service) industries involve the selling of services and skills, e.g. health service and transport.
4. **Quaternary** industries provide informations services, e.g. ICT and research.

(2) Key terms

- **Deindustrialisation** is the reduction of industrial activity in a particular region. Since the 1950s, the UK has become deindustrialised.
- **Globalisation** is the increased movement of goods and people between countries. It has created a more connected world and changed the UK's economy.

(10) Causes of economic change

Deindustrialisation

In the 1950s, about 35 per cent of people in the UK worked in the secondary sector. This percentage has declined sharply since. Reasons for deindustrialisation include:

- Machinery has increasingly replaced people.
- Globalisation has meant it is cheaper to import many products from abroad than produce them in the UK.
- Government polices like privatisation – selling off nationalised industries to private companies – resulted in a loss of jobs and a decline in UK traditional industry.

A post-industrial economy

The development of information technology has enabled a huge growth in service industries, particularly financial services. Email and video conferences allow UK companies to provide financial and business services to people around the world. Financial services generated 7 per cent of the UK's GDP in 2015. More science/business parks have been established and the number of people doing research jobs has increased. These parks have several businesses on one site, working in areas such as research and development, scientific research and business consultation. This has contributed to the growth of the quaternary sector.

(5) Worked example
Grades 3–4

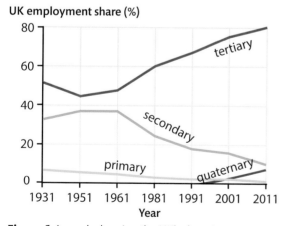

UK employment share (%)

Figure 1 A graph showing the UK's changing employment structure from the 1950s onwards

Study **Figure 1**. Describe the changes to the UK's employment structure since 1950. **[4 marks]**

Since 1950, there has been a large increase in the percentage of the UK workforce employed in the tertiary sector, and this period has also seen the emergence of the quaternary sector, which is growing rapidly.

Since 2000, more than 60 per cent of the workforce is employed in the tertiary sector. The percentage of people in the UK employed in the primary and secondary sectors has declined since 1950. Less than 20 per cent of the UK workforce is employed in primary and secondary industries.

(5) Exam-style practice
Grade 5

Explain how government policy has contributed to the decline in the primary and secondary sectors of the UK economy. **[4 marks]**

Made a start | Feeling confident | Exam ready

Impacts of industry

Industrial practices have had an impact on the UK's environment, but some modern industrial developments are becoming more environmentally sustainable. This is vital for a more sustainable future.

Environmental impacts of industry in the UK

Steel production, mining and quarrying in the UK impact the environment in the following ways:

- The process of extracting or manufacturing resources leads to air pollution. For example, in 2013, Tata Steel in Port Talbot, Wales, was ordered to stop pollution following the release of black dust around the residential areas near the plant.
- The transportation of both raw materials and manufactured products causes increased pollution from lorries.
- Industrial units scar the countryside, which ruins the beauty of the natural landscape. Operations can lead to disruption of natural systems including wildlife habitats.
- Disposal of industrial waste in landfill contaminates the landscape, polluting the soil and destroying wildlife habitats.

Named example

Tata Steel

You need to know an example of how modern industry can reduce its environmental impact and become more sustainable. This could be done by disposing of waste carefully to minimise soil and water pollution, recycling materials wherever possible, and making their processes more efficient so they use fewer raw materials.

Tata Steel is an example of how modern industrial development can be more sustainable. They have implemented several strategies to make their operations in the UK more sustainable, including the following:

1 In 2012, the company invested in a £55 million project to reduce its power requirements. This involved the introduction of a new waste heat recovery system. The increased efficiency of its operations has cut the energy consumption of their Port Talbot site by 15 per cent.

2 The company is a member of the Ultra-Low Carbon dioxide (CO_2) Steelmaking (ULCOS) partnership, along with 47 other European companies, which aims to reduce carbon dioxide emissions in steel production by at least 50 per cent by 2050.

3 Tata Steel regularly monitor water discharge for suspended solids and hydrocarbons to continually keep these pollutants at low levels. This has seen a reduction in hydrocarbon discharge of 15 per cent between 2009 and 2011.

Figure 1 New steel production technologies to reduce carbon dioxide emissions at Tata Steel plants

Worked example

Grades 4–6

Using a named example, explain how modern industry can be more environmentally sustainable. **[4 marks]**

Modern industries are investing in new technologies to reduce their impact on the environment. An example is Tata Steel, which has invested in reducing their carbon emissions through heat recovery systems. This helps to increase the efficiency of their steel production and they have reduced their energy consumption at their Port Talbot site by 15 per cent. Alongside the investment in new technologies, the company has committed to the Ultra-Low Carbon dioxide (CO_2) Steelmaking (ULCOS) partnership with other companies, with the ambition of helping to reduce carbon dioxide emissions in steelmaking by 50 per cent by 2050.

Exam-style practice

Grade 5

Suggest **one** impact of industry on the physical environment of the UK. **[2 marks]**

Rural landscape changes

You need to know the social and economic effects of population growth and decline in rural areas.

Population growth

Rural areas may grow for a number of reasons. Many rural areas, especially near the coast, are attractive to retired people. Villages in rural areas can also grow due to counter-urbanisation: people moving to rural areas and commuting to work in towns.

Northumberland

Northumberland is a rural area in the north-east of England with a growing population. According to government censuses, the population of Northumberland increased by 8838 people between 2001 and 2011.

Many of these were retired people: in 2011 20 per cent of the population in the area was aged 65 and over. These changes have social and economic effects.

Social and economic changes and effects

Social effects	Economic effects
Commuters are increasing traffic volume, which increases travelling times for locals.	Local services are struggling with the increasing numbers of migrants.
Pressures to build houses on green belt land leads to objections from local communities.	The unemployment rate is above the national average; increased competition for jobs.
Second homes can have a detrimental effect on communities.	The ageing population is putting increasing pressure on healthcare services.

Population decline

Reasons for a declining population in rural areas include:

- Loss of primary industries, such as mining and fishing, mean there are fewer jobs available.
- A decline in the availability of services, such as GP practices, can encourage people to move elsewhere.

The Outer Hebrides

The Outer Hebrides are a group of islands off the west coast of Scotland. Their population is predicted to decline by 13.7 per cent between 2014 and 2039, with the number of young people declining at a rapid rate. This would result in a population decrease from 27,250 in 2014 to 23,515 in 2039. The proportion of people over the age of 65 is expected to increase by 11 per cent during the same time period.

Social and economic changes and effects

Social effects	Economic effects
Schools face an uncertain future from a declining number of students.	The ageing population is putting increasing pressure on healthcare budgets.
There are fewer leisure and entertainment services aimed at young people.	Traditional sectors like the Harris Tweed industry are declining.
Breakdown of family units, with the younger generation migrating in search of better education and employment prospects.	The ageing population may increase the number of healthcare and service jobs available, but they may be low paid.

Worked example
Grades 2–4

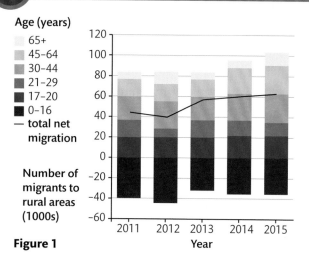

Figure 1

Study **Figure 1**, a chart showing net internal migration to rural areas by age band, in UK (from 2011 to 2015).

1 What was the total net migration in 2012?

[1 mark]

40,000

2 Suggest **one** reason why there is a net outward migration of 17–20 year olds. **[2 marks]**

This is when young people move from their home to higher education in more urban areas.

Exam-style practice
Grade 5

For a rural landscape you have studied, explain **one** social and **one** economic effect of population growth. **[4 marks]**

Made a start   Feeling confident   Exam ready

Infrastructure improvements

Population increase in the UK is putting pressure on transport infrastructure, leading to the need for improvements and new developments in road and rail infrastructure, and port and airport capacity to meet this demand. Better transport links can also help to create economic change and resolve regional differences.

(5) Smart motorways

Figure 1 New smart motorway section of the M25 with speed restrictions that can be altered remotely

Smart motorways use technology to actively manage the flow of traffic. A control centre remotely monitors traffic and activates signs to alert drivers to hazards or changes and to close lanes.

Smart motorways have been proven to reduce accidents, reduce traffic congestion and improve journey times. They are also cheaper to create and have less of an impact on the environment compared with adding extra lanes to motorways.

(5) Railway improvements

Figure 2 Railway worker improving the track

The number of rail journeys made each year doubled between 1997 and 2015, and is expected to double again by 2040. Several rail improvement schemes have been planned:

(1) Crossrail is a £14.8 billion project which involves the construction of a new rail line from the west to the east of London. It includes 10 new stations, and is designed to speed up journey times throughout the south-east.

(2) HS2 (High Speed 2) is a plan to provide a high speed link between the north and the south. The aim is to improve transport connections between key cities to promote economic growth.

(10) Port and airport capacity improvements

In 2012, the UK aviation sector contributed £52 billion to the UK's GDP, provided 960,000 jobs and generated £8.7 billion in taxation.

In 2016, a £344 million expansion to London City Airport was agreed. It will increase the number of people able to use the airports and the number of flights available. The project will also create 1600 new jobs at the airport and potentially contribute £1.5 billion to the UK economy by 2025.

UK port and airport developments

Liverpool is a £400 million investment to create a new deep-water container terminal at the Port of Liverpool, enabling the largest vessels to dock in this central UK location. This has generated new employment and boosted the local economy.

At the port of Felixstowe a new rail terminal was opened in 2013 to double the rail capacity of the UK's largest container port.

(5) Worked example   Grades 4–6

Give **two** benefits of improvements to road infrastructure in the UK. **[2 marks]**

One benefit is improvements to the flow of traffic during peak times. Another benefit is a reduction in the number of fatal accidents.

If you are asked to give two benefits for a 2 mark question, you don't need to develop your answer, just make accurate points, like in the answer shown.

(5) Exam-style practice   Grades 4–5

Suggest the benefits of improvements to rail networks in the UK. **[3 marks]**

The north–south divide

The north–south divide refers to the economic and cultural differences, including health statistics, house prices and political influence between southern England and the rest of the UK.

10 The divide

Deindustrialisation in the north of the UK and the growth of the service sector in the south have meant that the north has become poorer in comparison, while London and the south-east have developed rapidly. London is the main financial hub of the UK, and government spending on infrastructure is higher in the capital than in the north.

In April 2016, median full-time earnings in London were approximately £670 per week, compared with approximately £500 per week in the north-west and Yorkshire and the Humber. Unemployment rates in the north-east were 8.6 per cent for July–September 2015, which is 4.5 per cent higher than the south-east.

Government spending on infrastructure is significantly higher in London than anywhere else in the country. The average public spending on infrastructure per resident in London was £5426, compared with £502 in the south-east and £223 in the north-east.

Figure 1 A map showing what geographers believe to be the divide between the 'north' and the 'south' in the UK.
For example, in 2011, the life expectancy for women living in Cambridgeshire was 83.5 years compared with 79.2 years in Liverpool.

Describe the differences in quality of life between the north and south of the UK and give reasons why these differences have developed.

5 Resolving differences

- ✓ In 2016, the government launched the Northern Powerhouse strategy to help improve economic wealth in the north through increased investment in cities like Liverpool and Manchester.
- ✓ The HS2 plans (see page 69) are aimed at bridging the gap between the north and the south by improving rail transport links.
- ✓ Since 2011, a number of Enterprise Zones have been created to encourage the establishment of new businesses in the north by providing financial support, superfast broadband and more straightforward set-up regulations.

5 Worked example  Grades 2–3

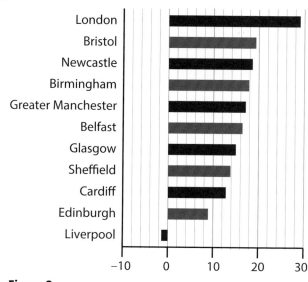

Figure 2

Study **Figure 2**, a chart showing percentage population growth for UK cities (2009–2014).

(a) What is the percentage growth for London?
[1 mark]

29 per cent

(b) What is the difference between the percentage growth for Birmingham and Edinburgh?
[1 mark]

9 per cent

2 Exam-style practice Grades 2–4

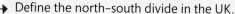

Define the north–south divide in the UK. **[2 marks]**

 Made a start **Feeling confident** **Exam ready**

The UK in the wider world

The UK has one of the largest economies in the world. You need to know the UK's place in the wider world in relation to trade, culture, transport, electronic communication, the European Union (EU) and the Commonwealth.

 UK connections with the world

Trade

Although the UK imports more products than it exports, in 2016 the UK was the world's 10th biggest exporter. In 2016, the top export destinations for UK goods were the USA, Germany and France. The UK imported the most from Germany, the USA and China.

> Imports are products that are brought into a country, whereas exports are products that a country sells to other countries.

Transport

By 2030, London is predicted to become a megacity, with the population expected to exceed 10 million. London's Heathrow airport is the UK's largest airport, which serves 194 destinations, and was used by 75.7 million people in 2016.

Electronic communication

The UK's digital communications infrastructure has significantly improved with the roll out of a superfast broadband network across the country. This helps to stimulate economic growth by increasing online spending and investment from companies overseas, and helps businesses to communicate globally and expand their operations worldwide.

Culture

Around 375 million people around the world speak English as their first language, and English is the most frequently studied foreign language in the world. The UK's cultural influence is expanding through sports, such as the 2012 London Olympics, and the distribution of successful television series such as *Downton Abbey*, which has been distributed in over 200 countries.

EU

The UK's decision to leave the EU will see a change in the UK's trading relationships and role in the global market. Membership of the EU previously affected the UK in several ways, including:

- The ability to trade within the single market, with members of the single market able to freely move goods and services between themselves.
- Free movement of migrant workers from member countries. For example, migrants from Poland, who moved to the UK in search of higher paid employment, contribute towards the UK's economy.
- The necessity to support other members through donations in the form of money, goods and services.

Between March 2016 and March 2017, there was more immigration to the UK by non-EU citizens than by EU citizens; approximately 264,000 non-EU citizens and 250,000 EU citizens immigrated to the UK.

The Commonwealth

The Commonwealth is a voluntary association of 52 countries across Africa, Asia, the Caribbean and Americas, Europe and the Pacific. They work together to promote human rights, peace, democracy and economic development. The Commonwealth has grown from eight members in 1949 to 52 members in 2017. Trade between the member countries is on average 19 per cent cheaper than trade between member countries and non-member countries because of similarities in legal systems and language.

 Worked example **Grades 2–4**

Explain the advantages of EU membership to the UK. **[4 marks]**

There are several advantages of EU membership to the UK. One economic advantage is being able to trade within the European single market, which makes importing goods to and from EU countries easier. In 2016, the country the UK imported the most from was Germany. Another advantage of EU membership is that skilled migrants from EU countries are able to easily work in the UK without a work permit. This benefits the healthcare profession; in 2015, nearly 20 per cent of NHS nurses were non-British, most of whom were from the EU...

 Exam-style practice **Grades 4–5**

Suggest how improvements in electronic infrastructure are increasing the UK's connections to the world. **[3 marks]**

 Made a start **Feeling confident** 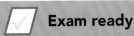 **Exam ready**

Types of resources

A resource is any physical material that is of value or purpose to people. Food, energy and water are fundamental resources for human development but their supply and consumption is not the same everywhere in the world.

(5) Three vital resources

1. **Fresh water** is vital for human survival, both for drinking and crop production.
2. **Food** is a vital resource because we need it to survive and we need a variety of nutrients to stay healthy.
3. **Energy** is vital for economic development, powering factories, transport, homes, businesses and schools.

(10) Global inequalities in supply and consumption

Water

One of the main causes of inequalities in water supply is the variation in amount of rainfall each country receives. For example, several countries in Africa receive very low amounts of rainfall and lack the infrastructure for storing and transporting water, leading to a **water deficit**. In contrast, Scotland, much of Wales and north-east England receive high amounts of rainfall and have the infrastructure to transfer water resources, leading to a **water surplus**.

Energy

As countries develop, their demand for energy increases. China, the USA and Russia are some of the biggest consumers of energy, much of which comes from fossil fuels. Most of China's energy comes from burning coal extracted within the country. Saudi Arabia produces and consumes a large quantity of oil per capita.

Food

People living in wealthy countries like the USA consume, on average, hundreds more calories per day in comparison with people living in poorer countries, such as Burkina Faso. In wealthy countries, people can afford to buy more food and there tends to be a better infrastructure for distributing food. There is also better access to transport, which makes it easier to buy food. The global consumption of food is very unevenly distributed, which is leading to obesity problems in some countries and undernourishment in others.

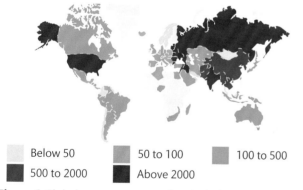

Below 50 | 50 to 100 | 100 to 500
500 to 2000 | Above 2000

Figure 1 Global energy consumption, including coal, gas, oil, electricity, heat and biomass, measured in million tonnes of oil equivalent (Mtoe)

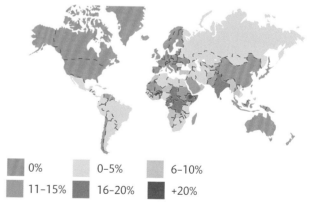

0% | 0–5% | 6–10%
11–15% | 16–20% | +20%

Figure 2 Percentage of the population who are undernourished

(5) Worked example · Grades 4–5

Suggest reasons for acute undernutrition in African countries. **[3 marks]**

Parts of Africa suffer from extreme poverty, which leads to undernutrition. Many people are too poor to obtain enough food and a lack of transport makes it difficult to access food markets. Poor infrastructure also makes it difficult to evenly distribute food supplies.

Exam focus

When asked to study a resource in the exam, use specific information from it to support your answer.

(5) Exam-style practice · Grades 3–4

Study **Figure 1**. Describe the distribution of countries which use more than 500 million tonnes of oil equivalent (Mtoe). **[2 marks]**

Food resources in the UK

As the UK's population continues to grow, there is an increasing demand for more food and a range of food types at affordable prices, which creates both opportunities and challenges.

(10) Food demand and supply

In recent years the demand for food in the UK has increased, driven by the growing population. This has made the food industry very lucrative: in 2014, total consumer expenditure on food, drink and catering was £198 billion. As a result, the provision of food resources in the UK is also changing.

High value imports and organic food

There is a growing demand in the UK for high value food exports, such as avocados and fine beans, from NEEs, such as Mexico, and LICs, such as Kenya. There is also a rising demand in the UK for fresh produce all year round. In 2012, the UK had a self-sufficiency rate (the ability to feed its population with what it produces) of only 58 per cent for vegetables and 11 per cent for fruits. Therefore, the UK imports many high-value food products from low income countries, where they are grown or produced, to meet this demand. Since 2000, there has also been a rise in the demand for organic produce in the UK, with sales increasing from £802 million in 2000 to £1.95 billion in 2015.

Food miles

All year round, there is an increasing demand for seasonal food products, such as asparagus and strawberries, and for products that cannot be grown in the UK's climate, such as rice. Therefore, they are imported from other countries. In 2014, 27 per cent of the food consumed in the UK was sourced from European Union countries. Some of these imported food products travel thousands of miles, referred to as 'food miles', to reach the UK.

Transporting food over long distances leads to increased carbon emissions. For example, sugar snap peas are transported 8782 kilometres from Guatemala via aeroplane, which releases more than 4500 g of greenhouse gases into the atmosphere. If consumers buy seasonal foods when they are available locally, it reduces food miles and carbon emissions.

Agribusinesses

Agribusinesses are the businesses involved in the production, sale and distribution of farming products. To meet the rising demand for low value food, many UK farms are run as businesses. Lynford House Farm, near Ely, is an example of an agribusiness. In order to be a sustainable business, the farm has put various measures in place to cut costs and increase profit. This includes sharing expensive machinery with other farms; securing external investment for the installation of a 54 million litre reservoir; joining with other local farmers to buy chemicals in bulk to reduce the cost by 20 per cent.

(5) Worked example — Grades 3–5

Suggest reasons why the UK imports food.

[3 marks]

One of the reasons why the UK imports food is the demand for a wider range of products, including organic produce and seasonal foods throughout the year. Another reason is the UK climate, which is not suitable for growing certain food products. Lastly, the UK's population is rising, increasing consumption and therefore the demand for food supplies.

Exam focus

If the question doesn't tell you how many points you need to give, look at how many marks it's worth to give you an idea of how long your answer needs to be.

(5) Exam-style practice — Grades 2–3

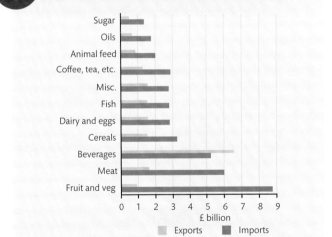

Figure 1 UK trade in different food groups (2014)

Study **Figure 1**, and answer the following questions.

(a) Suggest reasons for the value of the UK's imports and exports of coffee, tea and cocoa.

[4 marks]

(b) Calculate the difference between the imports and exports of dairy and eggs. **[1 mark]**

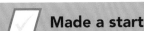

Water resources in the UK

Water is an essential resource for life, important for health and well-being, and necessary for agriculture and industry.

 Water demand and supply

People in the UK use about 150 litres of water a day. This value has been growing by 1 per cent a year since 1930 and will continue to rise as the population increases.

Water quality

The government and Environment Agency constantly monitor water quality for pollution and chemical levels, looking for things such as nitrates in the water.

It is particularly important to monitor water sources near farms and areas of industrial manufacturing as they are particularly prone to pollution. Farmers are encouraged to follow the Code of Good Agricultural Practice, which minimises the risk of causing water pollution.

Water sources can also be polluted by run-off from roads, which can contain dirt and salt used for gritting.

Areas of deficit and surplus

Water in the UK is mainly sourced from rivers, reservoirs and groundwater aquifers.

- The north and west of the UK experience a **water surplus**, where supply exceeds demand, because of low population densities and high rates of precipitation.
- The south and east of the UK experiences a **water deficit**, where demand exceeds supply, because of high population densities and low rates of precipitation.
- In south-east England there are serious levels of **water stress**, which means that demand exceeds supply.

Go to page 80 for more about groundwater aquifers.

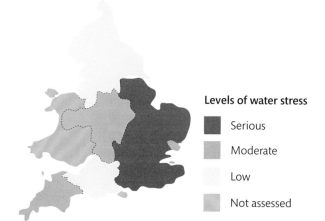

Levels of water stress

- Serious
- Moderate
- Low
- Not assessed

Figure 1 Water stress in areas of England and Wales

 Worked example   **Grades 4–6**

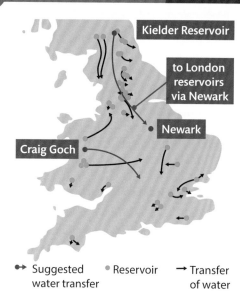

- ↔ Suggested water transfer
- • Reservoir
- → Transfer of water

Figure 2 Existing and suggested major water schemes in England and Wales

Study **Figure 2**. Describe the pattern of water transfer schemes and suggest a reason for their distribution across the UK.   **[4 marks]**

The map shows that existing local water transfer schemes in which water is only transferred a short distance are located around Leeds and Sheffield and in South Wales. It shows that the suggested long-distance water transfer schemes are transferring water from Wales to the midlands, and from the north to the midlands, such as the proposed transfer scheme from Kielder Reservoir near the border of Scotland, to the midlands. A likely reason for this is the water surplus in the north and west of the UK, and there is generally much less rainfall in the south-east, which can lead to water shortages and droughts.

 **Exam-style practice**   **Grades 2–3**

Study **Figure 1**. Describe the distribution of areas of serious and moderate water stress England and Wales.

   [2 marks]

 Made a start   **Feeling confident**   **Exam ready**

Energy resources in the UK

The UK is reducing its reliance on fossil fuels and increasing its use of renewable energy sources. This has created opportunities and challenges for the UK.

(10) The changing energy mix

Reliance on fossil fuels

The UK's reliance on coal (solid fuels) and oil (petroleum) has decreased since 1970, changing from a combined reliance of 91 per cent in 1970 to 50 per cent in 2014. However, there is an increasing reliance on gas because it is cheaper than oil. **Figure 1** shows the decline in coal use in the UK. UK coal mines have been driven to close by the rise of cheap imports and in response to concerns about the carbon dioxide emissions from coal-fired power stations.

Reduced supplies

In the UK, around 40 per cent of gas is used for heating and cooking in the home. This demand exceeds the domestic supply. The government predicts that by 2030 nearly three-quarters of natural gas used in the UK will be imported.

Renewable resources

Solar power, wind power and biomass are increasingly being used as alternatives to fossil fuels. Between July and September 2016, low carbon sources, such as wind turbines and nuclear power stations, accounted for 50 per cent of the UK's energy generation.

In 2015, 25 per cent of the UK's electricity came from renewable resources. The UK is on target to achieve its goal of meeting 15 per cent of its energy needs from renewables by 2020. This is helped by government incentives, which have encouraged a rise in the number of eco-homes fitted with improved insulation and energy efficient appliances.

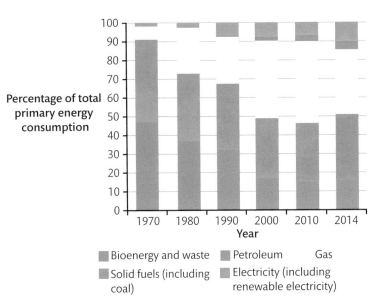

Figure 1 Total primary energy consumption by fuel, UK, 1970 to 2014

(5) Economic and environmental issues

The landscape is visually impacted.

Noise pollution is caused by turbines.

There is a potential impact on visitor numbers for tourist spots.

Wind energy

Transmission lines need to be built to bring the electricity to settlements.

Bird migration patterns may be disrupted.

Producing electricity is more expensive.

Nuclear waste requires careful management.

Nuclear energy

Power plants are expensive to build.

Damage to the power plants can cause leakage of dangerous substances.

(5) Worked example   Grades 5–6

Explain **two** environmental issues resulting from the exploitation of fossil fuels.   **[4 marks]**

One environmental issue from the exploitation of fossil fuels is that they are non-renewable resources, so they will eventually run out, meaning that using them is unsustainable. Another environmental issue is that extraction of fossil fuels, such as fracking for shale gas, can cause noise and air pollution, destroy wildlife habitats and spoil the beauty of natural landscapes.

(5) Exam-style practice   Grade 2

Study **Figure 1**. Describe the changes in the UK's oil consumption since 1970.   **[3 marks]**

Distribution of food

Global demand for food is rising as the global population increases. At present, food supply does not match the level of demand in some parts of the world, causing serious issues.

 Global patterns

Food consumption

The estimated worldwide average number of calories consumed per person per day has increased from 2358 in 1964 to 2940 in 2015. However, this does not reflect the large variations across the world as there still are millions of people who are undernourished. There is a calorie surplus in many HICs and a calorie deficit in many LICS. In 2015, the average calorie consumption per person in HICs was over 3400 calories per day. Whereas, in LICs, such as sub-Saharan Africa, the average per capita was less than 2400 calories per day.

By 2050, the demand for food is expected to have increased by between 59 per cent and 98 per cent. One of the reasons for this is the increasing world population. Another reason is that rising incomes in NEEs mean that people can afford to buy more dairy and meat products.

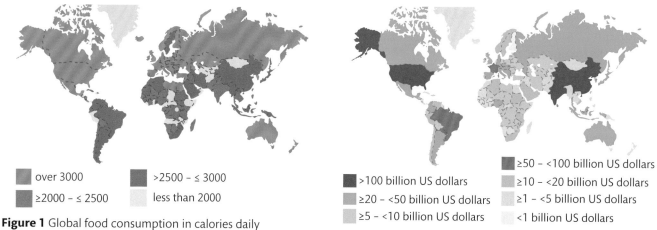

Legend (Figure 1):
- over 3000
- >2500 – ≤ 3000
- ≥2000 – ≤ 2500
- less than 2000

Figure 1 Global food consumption in calories daily

Legend (Figure 2):
- >100 billion US dollars
- ≥20 – <50 billion US dollars
- ≥5 – <10 billion US dollars
- ≥50 – <100 billion US dollars
- ≥10 – <20 billion US dollars
- ≥1 – <5 billion US dollars
- <1 billion US dollars

Figure 2 Global food production value, 2006

Food supply

Food supply is more secure in HICs so calorie consumption is higher. Wealthier countries can afford to import large amounts of food, and many HICs, like the USA, have high production levels due to intensive farming methods. Many LICs have a much lower average calorie consumption and a deficit of food because they cannot afford to produce or import large quantities of food. They tend to also have an extreme climate which makes it more difficult to grow crops.

 **Key factors affecting food supply**

- **Climate and weather** – rising temperatures and extreme weather events have a negative impact on crop yields.
- **Pests and diseases** – crop diseases and pests that destroy crops are becoming increasingly widespread as a result of the rising global temperatures.
- **Water scarcity** – a lack of reliable water supplies affects crop production and leads to food insecurity.
- **Conflicts** – conflicts can lead to the destruction of crops and ruined land, preventing future food production.
- **Technology** – advancements in technology improve crop yield and productivity. Examples include aeroponics (growing crops in misty environments) and hydroponics (growing crops in mineral solutions).
- **Poverty** – people living in poverty struggle to produce food because they cannot afford the equipment, technology or fertilisers.

Worked example — Grade 2

Give **two** reasons for increasing global food consumption. **[2 marks]**

Rising world population; increased affluence

Exam-style practice — Grade 6

Explain how global food insecurity can be reduced. **[6 marks]**

Impacts of food insecurity

Around the world, more than 800 million people are stricken by chronic undernourishment and food insecurity – not having a sufficient supply of nutritious food.

(15) The consequences of food insecurity

< 5% (very low)	5%–14.9% (moderately low)	15%–24.9% (moderately high)
25%–34.9% (moderately high)	35% and over (very high)	missing or insufficient data

Figure 1 Prevalence of undernourishment in the population (2014-2016)

Undernutrition

Undernutrition occurs when people do not have enough nutritious food for growth, energy and maintaining a healthy immune system, over a long period of time. It makes people more vulnerable to disease and illness.

Famine

Famine is a period of extreme scarcity of food, when more than 30 per cent of people in the affected area are acutely undernourished and when more than 2 people per 10,000 per day are dying because of lack of food.

Soil erosion

Soil erosion is caused by overgrazing, overcultivation and deforestation. In many African countries, food insecurity leads to subsistence farmers using land over and over again, eventually causing the land to become infertile and unusable. This is known as **overcultivation**.

Rising prices

When demand for food is high but the supply falls, the price increases. Rising food prices are leading to an increase in world hunger. For example, in the Philippines, rising rice prices are making it more difficult for people to afford to buy sufficient food and ultimately contributing to growing poverty.

Social unrest

Millions of people each year are affected by conflicts that lead to food insecurities. For example, about half of the people in Syria and Yemen are suffering from severe food insecurity. Sudden increases in food prices can also cause rioting and conflicts.

(5) Worked example   Grade 4

Other impacts include reduced capacity to work, and impaired physical and mental development in children.

Describe **one** impact of undernutrition.

[2 marks]

One impact of undernutrition is that people's immune systems may be weaker and they become more vulnerable to diseases.

(5) Exam-style practice   Grade 4

Give **two** impacts of food insecurity.   **[2 marks]**

Increasing food supply

You need to know the different strategies that can be used to increase food supply, including how new technology is being used, and the advantages and disadvantages of large agricultural developments.

Strategies for increasing food supply

Drip irrigation techniques are an efficient way to conserve water and lead to crop yield increases of 30–50 per cent. **Microtube irrigation systems**, which use the effects of gravity in connected small tubes to distribute water evenly to the roots of plants, are low cost and easy to install.

Biotechnology is the manipulation of biological processes, such as photosynthesis and resistance to insects and disease. It increases crop yields and produces more nutritious crops without deficiencies.

The new green revolution refers to the use of new technology to increase the production of food. Techniques include: developing new seed varieties to grow in specific conditions, soil conservation (the prevention of soil loss from erosion and reduced fertility) and rainwater harvesting.

Increasing food supply

Aeroponics involves growing plants in a mist environment without the use of soil. The roots are suspended, allowing them to access more oxygen and grow faster. They are sprayed with a fine mist of water and/or nutrient solution. This increases yields and reduces costs.

Hydroponics involves growing plants in mineral nutrient solutions rather than soil. It can increase global food supply because plants can be grown in regions where there is no fertile soil.

Appropriate technology is designed to be suitable for a location and for the farmers using it. For example, in drought prone areas farmers use 'traditional' water conservation techniques and planting methods, such as the Zai system used in West Africa. Farmers fill small holes with manure, which attracts termites that build underground tunnels. The tunnels capture water and recycle soil nutrients.

Named example

The Indus Basin Irrigation System

The Indus Basin Irrigation System in Pakistan is the largest irrigation system of its kind in the world. It includes three large dams, 85 small dams and 12 inter-river linking canals. Agricultural products from this area constitute 23 per cent of Pakistan's GDP, but there are advantages and disadvantages to the irrigation system.

Advantages and disadvantages of the Indus Basin Irrigation System

Advantages	Disadvantages
👍 More hydroelectric power is produced.	👎 It has increased the amount of groundwater, which has led to waterlogging. Waterlogged soil is less useful for agriculture.
👍 Improved yields of crops, including rice, vegetables and sugarcane, due to better access and water supplies for irrigation from the Mangla and Tarbela reservoirs. This has improved food supply and incomes in Pakistan.	👎 Sedimentation can reduce the amount of water that can be stored.
👍 A wider range of food products can be grown.	👎 Farmers can be deprived of water further downstream.
👍 Opportunities for fishing in the Mangla and Tarbela reservoirs provide an additional source of food and have improved the diet of local people.	👎 The population within the basin is projected to increase, putting increasing pressure on water availability.

Exam focus

Remember to revise the named example you have studied in class. You should try to remember points that are specific to the example you have learned.

  Exam-style practice **Grade 4**

Using a specific example, describe the advantages of a large-scale agricultural development project.

[4 marks]

 Made a start **Feeling confident** **Exam ready**

Sustainable food options

You need to know the ways in which food supplies can become more sustainable. You also need to know details about a large scale agricultural development, including its advantages and disadvantages.

Sustainable food supplies

Organic farming involves using natural techniques instead of chemicals to grow crops and rear livestock. Some chemicals have a negative impact on soil health and pollinating insects. This method of farming tends to be less efficient and have a higher cost, but it is more sustainable.

Permaculture simulates or directly uses features of an ecosystem to improve crop yield. Examples include biofertilisers, holistic grazing and agroforestry. It is a sustainable and non-polluting approach .

Urban farming initiatives refers to the production of food in and around urban areas. An example is the GrowUp Box in London, which uses upcycled shipping containers, aquaponics and vertical growing technologies to produce sustainable supplies of fresh fish, salads and herbs.

Sustainable food supplies

Reducing waste is essential to making food supplies more sustainable. In 2015, the UK produced 4.4 million tonnes of edible household food waste. The UK government is aiming for a 'zero waste economy' where all waste is reduced, reused or recycled.

Seasonal consumption of locally grown fruit and vegetables helps to reduce 'food miles', lowering carbon emissions. It also supports the livelihood of local farmers.

Sustainably sourced fish and meat requires regulation. Many governments set quotas to prevent overfishing to maintain fish species for future generations. Responsibly sourced meat is produced by small-scale farms that use free range and organic methods.

Worked example — Grade 4

Figure 1 A rooftop vegetable garden

Study **Figure 1**. Describe how the scheme shown can increase sustainable supplies of food.

[2 marks]

Figure 1 shows an example of an urban farming initiative. This can help make food supplies more sustainable as it increases the amount of food available in urban areas, where many people live, which reduces food miles and carbon emissions.

Named example

Rwanda Aid

- In Rwanda around 85 per cent of the population survive on subsistence farming. Most farmers own less than a hectare of land, with infertile soils on steep slopes.
- Rwanda Aid works in partnership with the local communities, providing training in sustainable organic farming. This involves the use of compost, mulch, new crops, crop rotation and soil conservation. More than 800 people have been trained so far.
- Rwanda Aid has helped to improve crop production and has enabled farmers to create an income from their produce.

Exam-style practice — Grade 4

1 Explain how food supplies can be made more sustainable. **[6 marks]**

2 Using an example you have studied, give **one** advantage and **one** disadvantage of a large scale agricultural development. **[2 marks]**

Distribution of water

Water security can be defined as the ability to access sufficient quantities of good quality fresh water for health, livelihoods and production. Global demand for water is increasing, but supply can be unreliable, leading to water insecurity.

 Why is water consumption increasing?

Population increase and economic development are the main reasons water consumption is rising. The world's population is growing by approximately 80 million people per year, and changes to lifestyles and eating habits have increased the rate of water consumption per person.

The rising demand for food due to global population growth and economic development is also causing water consumption to increase. Water is required for the irrigation of crops, food production and cooking. Economic development means people have more money to spend on food, which is leading to changes in diets. Meat and dairy products, which require a lot of water to produce, are becoming increasingly popular.

The growing use of biofuels is also increasing the demand for water. Producing one litre of biofuel from corn requires around 2000 litres of water.

By 2025, it is estimated that 460 million people will live in water-stressed countries, where the demand for water exceeds the amount available. Severe water shortages already affect an estimated 2.7 billion people worldwide.

 What factors affect water availability?

- **Climate and weather** – global and annual variations in climate and weather affect water availability both within and between countries. For example, a high volume of rainfall and a mild climate will lead to a water surplus.
- **Geology** – some countries extract and use water from aquifers. Aquifiers are underground areas of porous rock that store groundwater.
- **Pollution** – industry and farming have led to the pollution of rivers. Polluted water often contains harmful bacteria making it unfit for human consumption.
- **Over-abstraction** – some countries, such as Mexico, are **abstracting** (extracting) too much water from aquifers before it can be replenished. This has resulted in severe water shortage problems in Mexico City.
- **Limited infrastructure** – a lack of piped water in LICs and NEEs limits the supply to remote villages.
- **Poverty** – LICs do not usually have enough money to pay for mains water supplies. People tend to share communal water sources, like rivers and streams, which can be polluted and therefore a health-risk.

 Worked example Grades 3–4

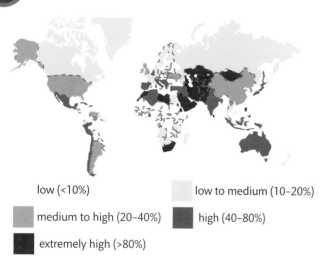

low (<10%)
low to medium (10–20%)
medium to high (20–40%)
high (40–80%)
extremely high (>80%)

Figure 1 Water stress by country, 2013

Study **Figure 1**. Describe the distribution of areas of extremely high water stress and low water stress.

[3 marks]

The areas of extremely high water stress are nearly all in North Africa or the Middle East, with the exception of Mongolia, which is a country with extremely high water stress in Asia. Many of the areas of low water stress are in tropical regions in Asia and Central and South America. Much of Africa has low water stress, with the exception of countries in the north and south. There are also several eastern and northern European countries with low water stress.

Water stress refers to the amount of water available per person, so water stress by country is affected by population as well as climate.

 Exam-style practice Grade 5

Explain the reasons why water consumption is increasing. **[4 marks]**

Impacts of water insecurity

Water is vital for ecosystems and humans to survive, but most of the water systems currently in place have become stressed, causing social, economic and environmental impacts.

(10) Social, economic and environmental impacts

Waterborne diseases/pollution

Waterborne diseases from polluted water sources affect more than 1.5 billion people every year. Many people in African and some Asian countries are forced to drink contaminated water, leading to diseases, such as cholera and dysentery. These water resources are contaminated from poor industrial practices and a lack of basic sanitation.

Conflict

Rising demands for water and uncertain supplies are causing social unrest in some of the most affected regions, like the Middle East and North Africa. Water insecurity may lead to violence. For example, Turkey is able, through its dams, to affect the water supply in countries further downstream in the Tigris-Euphrates basin, such as Syria, Egypt and Iraq, which could cause unrest.

Impacts of water insecurity

Industrial output

Water is essential to industrial processes. The production of one pair of jeans requires around 6800 litres of water. Water is also necessary for processes used to generate electricity. This means that water shortages can lead to a reduction in manufacturing. In 2016 in India, the poor monsoon seasons in the two years before led to reduced production of paper products and textiles. Reduced industrial output also has a negative effect on a country's economy.

Food production

Water is key to food security because agriculture requires large amounts of water. The production of one kilogram of beef requires over 15,000 litres. Periods of drought can lead to problems with crop production, leading to a reduction in global food supplies. By 2050, crop yields across sub-Saharan Africa may decline by 5–22 per cent due to droughts, while countries in West Africa may be able to grow more food as rainfall increases and temperatures rise. North-east Brazil could see a soya crop yield decrease of more than 20 per cent, while as a whole Latin America's potatoes and quinoa yields could rise.

Other impacts of water insecurity include conflicts (social) and reduced manufacturing (economic and social).

You could include social, environmental or economic impacts in your answer.

(2) Key terms

- ☑ **Water insecurity** – When there is not enough good quality safe water available for people to be healthy and productive.
- ☑ **Water conservation** – The control and development of resources to use less water and prevent pollution.
- ☑ **Over-abstraction** – When water is being used more quickly than it is being replaced.

(10) Worked example — Grades 5–7

Discuss the impacts of water insecurity.

[6 marks]

Water insecurity can lead to several impacts on people and the environment. One example is a decrease in the global production of food caused by changes to climatic conditions, such as rising temperatures and longer periods of droughts. This could result in increases in the prices of key staple crops, such as rice and wheat, as less become available. Water insecurity can also lead to waterborne diseases as a direct result of a lack of infrastructure in many LICs. Many remote villages rely on water sources that are polluted as a result of poor sanitation and industrial waste. Drinking contaminated water can lead to the contraction of diseases, like cholera, and illnesses, such as dysentery.

(5) Exam-style practice — Grade 4

Suggest how water insecurity can cause conflict.

[3 marks]

Increasing water supply

The global demand for fresh water is rising as the world's population expands. You need to know the different strategies that can be used to increase the supply of water.

 Strategies to increase water supply

Diverting supplies and increasing storage

Water transfer involves the movement of water from an area of surplus to an area of deficit, using extensive pipelines. An example is the Kielder Transfer Scheme in Northumberland, UK. Kielder Water is the largest man-made lake

Figure 1 Kielder Water

in northern Europe and can hold 200 billion litres of water. When river levels are low, water is released from this reservoir into nearby rivers. The benefits of Kielder include a plentiful supply of water to the north-east and the creation of jobs. However, the scheme has had negative impacts, including the loss of farmland and the disruption of river ecosystems.

Dams and reservoirs

A dam is a barrier that controls a river's flow and stores water upstream in a reservoir. This provides a store of water for both domestic and agricultural use. It also provides protection from flooding further down the river by controlling the amount of water released. However, dams can have negative effects on the biological, chemical and physical properties of a river, for example, increasing erosion downstream and blocking fish migration routes.

Desalination

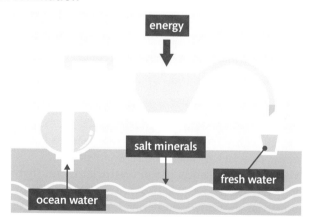

Figure 2 Desalination involves forcing water through special filters that trap the salt and impurities from seawater and convert it into fresh water.

The United Arab Emirates, an extremely arid area of the Middle East, has invested in building desalination plants. Desalination plants are expensive and the process contributes towards increasing carbon emissions.

 Named example

The South–North Water Diversion Project, China

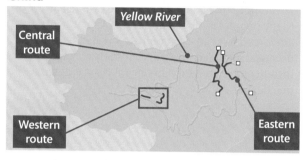

 waterway routes

Figure 4 A map showing the location of the pipelines for the South–North Water Diversion Project in China

This water transfer project is the biggest inter-basin scheme in the world. It involves transferring water from the south of China, which has high levels of rainfall, over 1000 km to the drier north-east, which has the highest population density in the country.

Advantages

- It has the potential to provide 44.8 billion cubic metres of fresh water per year from the Yangtze River in southern China to the north.
- It provides a more reliable source of water for the northern half of the country.
- It improves water supplies for agriculture and industry, leading to increase crop yields and productivity.

Disadvantages

- By completion in 2014, the project had cost over $79 billion.
- It resulted in the relocation of around 330,000 people.
- It is likely to cause disruption to wildlife.
- Parts of south China have experienced severe droughts in recent years, leading to failed harvests and a lack of drinking water.

Other disadvantages of reservoirs include the large volumes of methane they produce and the disruption to local people who are forced to relocate.

 Exam-style practice **Grade 5**

Using an example you have studied, explain **one** advantage and **one** disadvantage of a large-scale water transfer scheme.

[4 marks]

 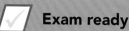

Sustainable water options

Fresh water needs to be managed sustainably to help tackle increasing water stress. You need to know the options available for sustainable water management as well as a named example of a local scheme in an LIC or NEE.

 Sustainable water options

'Grey' water is water from bathroom sinks, showers and washing machines. While it may contain traces of dirt, food or grease, it is ideal to use as a source of irrigation water for gardens.

Water conservation involves adopting ways to limit waste. These include:
· turning taps off when brushing teeth
· installing a low-flush toilet
· washing only full loads of clothes
· regularly checking for leakages
· installing a smart meter
· using low-flow shower heads.

Sustainable water options

Recycling involves the reuse of treated water. An example is Walkers who recycle water from one stage of the production process to use it in another stage. The Indian government has also invested in recycling plants to treat billions of litres of waste water every day.

Groundwater management is monitoring the quality of water under the surface of the Earth, as well as use of that water. In Santa Clara, California, a groundwater management plan has been in place for over 80 years to maintain the water source for domestic use.

 Named example

WaterAid in Vimphere

Local schemes organised by NGOs, like WaterAid, are vital for providing people in LICs and NEEs with a reliable source of water. Residents of the village of Vimphere, in Malawi, have been struggling to fetch water for a long time, due in part to the surrounding rocky hills and the Kasungu mountain range that make it hard to dig deep wells to access water underground. Most women and children spent hours queuing for water from a spring, even though this water was polluted.

WaterAid brought in a drilling rig to access the water underground, and it installed a pump for the village.

The villagers now have access to safe water, which has reduced the potential for people to contract waterborne diseases and illnesses like cholera and dysentery. It also means that children can go to school rather than spend hours fetching water.

Figure 1 Residents gathering around the drilling rig in Vimphere, Malawi

 Worked example Grades 2–3

What is water conservation? **[1 mark]**

Water conservation is the sustainable management of fresh water by adopting approaches to limit waste water.

 Exam-style practice Grade 5

Explain why local schemes to improve water supplies are important for people living in LICs and NEEs.

[4 marks]

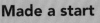

Distribution of energy

Demand for energy resources is rising globally. You need to know the factors that influence the distribution of energy supply and consumption.

 ## Global distribution of energy supply and consumption

China and the USA are the top two energy consuming countries in the world, with growing demands for both industrial and domestic use. If a country's energy supply exceeds its demand, such as in Canada, there is an **energy surplus**, whereas if the energy demand exceeds supply, such as in many areas of Asia, there is an **energy deficit**.

Global energy consumption is predicted to continue rising at approximately 2 per cent per year, which is the equivalent to the doubling of consumption every 35 years.

Why is energy consumption increasing?

The world's population is expected to increase by 2.2 billion to 9.7 billion by 2050. Larger populations consume more energy.

The economic growth in newly emerging economies increases the demand for energy in both the domestic and industrial sectors. As economies, such as India and China, grow and wealth increases, people have more money to buy electrical products and cars, all of which require energy, whilst expanding industry also leads to increased energy consumption.

Advances in technology are increasing the number and types of products available, all of which require energy to build, transport and use.

What factors affect energy supply?

- **Physical factors** – countries with optimal climatic and weather conditions can generate more energy from solar farms, hydroelectric dams and wind farms. Some countries have an abundance of fossil fuels and geothermal energy resources. For example, due to Iceland's location in a tectonically active area with many volcanoes, the country has plenty of geothermal energy available.

- **Cost of exploitation and production** – some countries don't have the money to extract resources or build oil or geothermal pipelines.

- **Technology** – some countries have invested in new technologies, which has enabled the extraction of new resources, such as shale gas through fracking.

- **Political** – unrest in oil-rich areas creates obstacles to the successful extraction and export of energy.

Worked example   Grades 1–3

18 per cent	
17 per cent	
16 per cent	
15 per cent	
10 per cent	

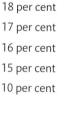

Using **Figure 1**, identify the percentage of energy generated from biomass in the province of Sichuan. Shade **one** circle only.   **[1 mark]**

A 18 per cent   ○

B 16 per cent   ◉

C 10 per cent   ○

Figure 1 Percentage of energy generated from biomass in China (2014)

Exam-style practice   Grade 5

Describe the factors that affect energy supply.

[4 marks]

Made a start   Feeling confident   Exam ready

Impacts of energy insecurity

Access to energy supplies is vital for social and economic development in modern economies. However, rising demand is leading to energy insecurity, which can have economic, social and environmental impacts.

(10) Social, economic and environmental impacts

Exploration of environmentally sensitive areas
The increasing demand for energy has led to the exploration of remote and environmentally sensitive areas to locate fossil fuels. Exploration and drilling for oil and gas in fragile environments, such as the Arctic, disrupts wildlife habitats. In particular, drilling disturbs fish and animals that are key to the livelihoods of indigenous people. Drilling for oil can also lead to spills that are difficult to contain and clean up, particularly in icy water (although new approaches are presently being researched). Response to an oil spill, even in ice-free periods, can take days or weeks due to the difficult conditions and the long distances involved. There are also economic implications of exploiting the Arctic for energy. Construction and operation of facilities in the Arctic is expensive, as is exporting the resource once extracted.

Industrial output
Energy is essential for food production, mineral extraction, industrial production and transportation. Countries that suffer from an inconsistent supply of energy resources experience delays in production lines or even closure, which has a significant impact on the economy.

Impacts of energy insecurity

Food production
Rapid changes to farming methods, such as the use of fertilisers, pesticides, machinery and irrigation systems, has caused a significant increase and reliance on energy to produce our food. Uncertainty over the availability of fossil fuels in the future could see a reduction in the availability of certain crops and foodstuffs that require a lot of energy to produce. This will lead to significant increases in the price of food.

Conflict
Many countries rely on imported fossil fuels, such as oil. Political unrest in recent years in the Middle East, a key global provider of oil, and the conflict in Ukraine, have created uncertainties around supplies and market prices. Future wars will likely be caused by the desire to control valuable oil and natural gas assets.

(10) Worked example
Grades 5–7

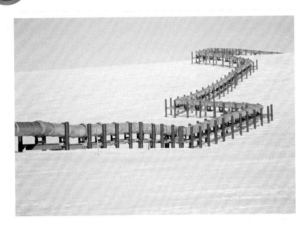

Figure 1 Oil pipeline in Alaska, USA

You could include social, environmental or economic impacts in your answer.

Using **Figure 1**, explain the impacts of energy insecurity. **[6 marks]**

Energy insecurity impacts on humans, the environment and the economy. For example, the exploration and extraction of fossil fuels in environmentally sensitive areas, such as the Arctic, destroys wildlife habitats and disrupts fish migration. This has a negative impact on indigenous people who rely on fishing as a source of sustenance and income.

Reliance on energy for the harvesting of crops means that energy insecurity also impacts on global food production. Uncertain supplies of fossil fuels lead to a reduction in the availability of crops, like wheat and rice, and an increase in global prices of food which require a lot of energy to produce, like meat.

(5) Exam-style practice
Grade 4

Suggest how energy insecurity can cause conflict. **[3 marks]**

Increasing energy supply

There are a variety of different strategies to increase energy supply, which can be categorised as renewable or non-renewable. You need to know the different strategies, as well as an example of the advantages and disadvantages of fossil fuel extraction.

 Renewable and non-renewable sources of energy

Renewable resources

Renewable resources include biomass, wind, solar, hydro, tidal, geothermal and wave energy. Worldwide, the percentage of energy sourced from renewables is increasing. In 2014, solar and wind energy accounted for 4 per cent of energy generation, but the World Energy Council predict that they could provide up to 39 per cent by 2060.

👍 The greatest advantage of renewable energy sources is that, unlike fossil fuels, they are not a finite resource so they won't run out.

👎 Renewable energy sources are dependent on location; for example, solar panels need lots of sunshine to generate energy.

Although renewable sources of energy generally produce less greenhouse gases than fossil fuels, they nevertheless have environmental impacts; for example, production of biomass takes up land that could be used for growing food crops, and wind turbines may kill or injure birds.

Non-renewable resources

Fossil fuels and nuclear power are non-renewable resources because oil, coal, gas, (fossil fuels) and uranium (used in nuclear power stations) will all eventually run out. In 2014, fossil fuels were the main source of energy, making up 81 per cent of the world's energy supply.

👍 They are often relatively cheap sources of energy.

👎 Burning fossil fuels produces large amounts of CO_2, which contributes to the greenhouse effect.

5 **Named example**

Oil extraction at Athabasca tar sands, Alberta, Canada

Advantages

👍 It provides employment for 514,000 people in Canada.

👍 It provides a secure source of energy for Canada.

👍 It boosts the economy of the province of Alberta, particularly through the export of oil to the USA.

Disadvantages

👎 Oil leaks caused by damaged pipelines have polluted the Athabasca River and the groundwater. This has had a negative impact on wildlife habitats and on people living nearby.

👎 The forest that grows over the oil reserves must be cleared, leading to the removal of local habitats and the release of carbon dioxide (CO_2).

👎 Bitumen refinement and the fuel produced from it release very large amounts of CO_2.

Figure 1 Suncor tar sands mine, Athabasca tar sands, Alberta, Canada

2 **Worked example** **Grade 3**

Give **two** ways energy supplies can be increased.
[2 marks]

By building more hydroelectric dams and by building more solar farms in sunny places

5 **Exam-style practice** **Grade 5**

Using an example you have studied, explain **one** advantage and **one** disadvantage of extracting a fossil fuel. **[4 marks]**

Sustainable energy options

You need to know about different sustainable energy options, as well as a named example of a local renewable energy scheme in an LIC or an NEE.

(10) Sustainable energy options

Fossil fuel efficiency
Improved transport technology is reducing fuel consumption for road, rail and air. Cars are now more aerodynamic and engine efficiency has improved, meaning cars can travel further per litre of fuel than they used to be able to.
Many governments are investing in sustainable transport schemes, such as the highly successful bike sharing schemes in Hangzhou, China and Copenhagen, Denmark.

Sustainable energy options

Energy conservation in the workplace
Hotels are adopting a 'no wash' policy for towels unless customers specifically ask for it during their stay. This reduces the number of washes the hotel does, and therefore the amount of energy used.
Many companies are providing employees with recycling facilities and encouraging them to dispose of their waste responsibly.
Video conferencing reduces the need for face-to-face meetings that require long distance travel.

Energy conservation at home
Individuals can reduce their energy consumption in the home by adopting some of the following: cavity wall and loft insulation; energy-efficient light bulbs; double glazing; using energy suppliers who use renewable energy; and using energy efficient appliances.

Individual use/carbon footprints
Individuals can take steps to reduce their own carbon footprints. This can involve car sharing, using public transport, recycling, buying local produce and reducing waste. These measures will contribute towards reducing carbon emissions.

(5) Named example

Belo Monte Dam, Brazil
The Belo Monte Dam is a local renewable energy scheme in Brazil, an NEE, that is intended to provide the country with a sustainable supply of energy. The dam is part of a wider programme of sustainable energy development in Brazil; the government has been investing in solar and wind power in recent years, as well as hydroelectricity.

When complete it will be the fourth largest hydroelectric dam in the world, and it will be able to generate over 11,000 MW of power.

Figure 1 The planned location of the Belo Monte Dam, a hydroelectric dam currently under construction on the Xingu River, a major tributary of the Amazon

Advantages
👍 It will help to satisfy the huge demand for energy in Brazil; the energy generated by the dam could power around 20 million homes.

👍 It provides job opportunities, both while it is under construction and after it has been completed.

👍 It can lead to improved infrastructure in the area, for example, wooden stilt houses in Altamira.

Disadvantages
👎 Flooding the Amazon rainforest will disrupt the ecosystem and potentially destroy animal and plant species.

👎 Diverting the Xingu River may lead to problems further downstream, such as migration patterns and sediment deposition.

👎 It is expected to disrupt the lives of 12,000 indigenous people who live nearby.

(2) Worked example — Grades 1–2

What is energy conservation? **[1 mark]**

Energy conservation is reducing energy consumption by individuals or organisations through adopting approaches to limit the wastage of energy.

(5) Exam-style practice — Grade 5

1 Explain strategies for sustainable energy use. **[4 marks]**

2 Outline **one** advantage and **one** disadvantage of a local renewable energy scheme in an LIC or NEE you have studied. **[2 marks]**

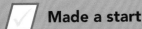 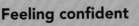

Pages **14–15,**
LINKS

Making geographical decisions

You will need to apply your understanding and knowledge of geography environments to make decisions about real-life situations.

 Worked example   **Grades 5–9**

'Rapid economic development leads to more problems than benefits.'

Do you agree with this statement?

Yes   No ⦿

Justify your decision.

[9 marks] [+ 3 SPaG marks]

There has been rapid economic development in India in recent decades, with a growth in the service sector that has seen India become a global leader in outsourcing highly-skilled workers. One of the main benefits of rapid economic growth is the rise in the country's GDP. By 2014, India had the seventh largest economy (based on GDP) in the world. One of the factors driving this was the removal of trade barriers during the 1990s, which resulted in a rise in both imports and exports. By 2013, exports were worth $337 billion. This has enabled India to invest in new infrastructure. However, most of the development has been focused on a few states.

Another benefit is the increase in the number and variety of jobs available. In India, the secondary sector, the tertiary sector, and parts of the quaternary sector have grown whilst the primary sector has declined, so a greater percentage of the population are employed in skilled and generally better-paid jobs than they were before. Manufacturing industries in particular have expanded considerably helped by government initiatives, such as Make in India. However, this has had negative environmental impacts, as it has contributed to India's increased energy use and carbon dioxide emissions...

In conclusion, it is clear from the case of India that rapid economic development brings both problems and benefits. Whilst the benefits of rapid economic development, such as a rise in the country's GDP and better employment opportunities, are considerable, they are outweighed by the social and environmental problems caused by development. Air and water pollution negatively impact upon the population's quality of life and increased carbon dioxide emissions contribute to global warming...

Exam focus

When you are asked to 'justify' this means you will need to support your opinion with accurate evidence. Remember to revise key facts and statistics about the case studies and named examples you have studied in class.

Make it clear in your opening paragraph which country you are considering and the reasons for choosing it.

The question refers to problems and benefits of rapid economic development, so you need to provide at least one example of both. (AO1)

Include specific facts and figures in your answer to support points.

Use specific examples, such as India's exports, and specialist terminology (infrastructure) to demonstrate that you have detailed knowledge and understanding about the topic. (AO2)

In your conclusion you should make a balanced decision about a whether you agree or disagree with the statement, summarising points from your answer to support your view. (AO3)

 Exam-style practice   **Grades 5–9**

'Hard engineering strategies are more beneficial to protecting coastlines than soft engineering strategies.'

Do you agree with this statement?

Yes   No

Justify your decision.

[9 marks] [+ 3 SPaG marks]

✓ **Made a start**   ✓ **Feeling confident**   ✓ **Exam ready**

Page 52 LINKS

Issue evaluation

In Paper 3, you will be expected to draw on your knowledge and understanding of both physical and human topics to answer questions based on topical issues.

② What is issue evaluation?

You will be tested on a theme from one of the core topics. You will be expected to draw on knowledge from both physical and human elements of your GCSE Geography course, and to demonstrate the interrelationships between the two areas.

12 weeks before the exam, you will receive a resource booklet to allow you to become familiar with the themes and resources. You can annotate this but will be issued a clean copy for the actual exam. There will also be resources in the exam paper in relation to contexts you have not seen before.

⑤ Using the booklet

Once you have received your resource booklet, take time to familiarise yourself with the sources and issues.

To prepare for the exam, try to follow these steps:

1 Review each source and consider which apsects of physical environments are relevant and which apsects of human environments are relevant.

2 Draw out any specific physical and human aspects from each source and consider how they relate to each other.

3 Look for conflicts or differing points of view within the sources. Decide whether you agree with one over another and create an evidence bank.

⑤ Key skills

☑ Interpret and analyse a geographical issue from seen and unseen resources.

☑ Make a decision based on your own knowledge and the sources provided.

☑ Justify your decision with evidence from the resources – remember, answers not supported with evidence will receive lower marks.

☑ Check that you have provided a balanced argument.

Include details from the sources or information from your own knowledge to support your decision.

⑤ Worked example   Grade 5

As the world's population continues to grow, the demand for water increases, putting increasing pressure on the freshwater resources available. Over 798 million people are without clean water, along with approximately 2.5 billion people who don't have adequate sanitation.

Look at **Figure 1**. What is the percentage of the population in Mozambique using an improved source of drinking water in 2015?

Shade **one** circle only.

[1 mark]

A   More than 80 per cent   ○

B   Less than 60 per cent   ◉

C   Between 60–80 per cent   ○

less than 60%   more than 80%

no data available

Figure 1 The percentage of the population in African countries using an improved source of drinking water

Exam focus

At the beginning of the issue evaluation questions, you will be presented with several shorter response questions, similar to the question shown here. You will be expected to extract evidence from the resources provided.

⑤ Exam-style practice   Grade 5

Study **Figure 1**. Suggest **one** reason for the variations in access to clean water sources in Africa.

[2 marks]

Using written sources

You will need to be able to use a range of different sources in the pre-release booklet, looking at what evidence it provides for the presented issue. Use this page to understand how to interpret and use some of the resources.

 Different types of sources

You may have to read several articles or information boxes that contain a range of different facts, figures and images related to a particular issue. The resource booklet will contain several longer resources and you might need to draw on information from different parts of one source.

Figure 1

Water problems around the world – improving access to sanitation

The World Health Organisation (WHO)

2.1 billion people lack safe drinking water at home, more than twice as many lack safe sanitation

Some 3 in 10 people worldwide, or 2.1 billion, lack access to safe, readily available water at home, and 6 in 10, or 4.5 billion, lack safely managed sanitation, according to a new report by WHO and UNICEF.

Billions of people have gained access to basic drinking water and sanitation services since 2000, but these services do not necessarily provide safe water and sanitation. Many homes, healthcare facilities and schools also still lack soap and water for handwashing.

Of the 4.5 billion people who do not have safely managed sanitation, 2.3 billion still do not have basic sanitation services. This includes 600 million people who share a toilet or latrine with other households, and 892 million people – mostly in rural areas – who defecate in the open. Due to population growth, open defecation is increasing in sub-Saharan Africa and Oceania...

Photograph A

 Worked example | **Grades 5–7**

1 Study **Figure 1**. Suggest how limited access to sanitation might affect the health of rural populations. **[2 marks]**

Many rural areas have growing populations which puts more strain on sanitation facilities. This is more likely to lead to the spread of diseases.

> Find the relevant information from the source text and develop it by suggesting the impact it has on the lives of people. Sanitation is often linked to health care.

2 Suggest why people living in rural areas might be more vulnerable to disease than those in urban areas. Use **Figure 1** and **Photograph A**, as well as your own understanding to support your answer. **[6 marks]**

Figure 1 states that 892 million people, mostly in rural areas, defecate in the open due to a lack of proper sanitation infrastructure. Photograph A shows people taking dirty water from a river or waterhole, which may be polluted with waste and chemicals from agriculture and industry. It is likely to contain a lot of bacteria. People in many rural areas are forced to drink water from sources like this, and are therefore vulnerable to diseases such as dysentery and cholera. Urban areas tend to have better access to clean water and safely managed sanitation facilities, due to better infrastructure, such as sewer systems and household water supplies...

> You need to identify, describe and interpret what you can be see in the photo.

 Exam-style practice | **Grade 5**

Using **Figure 1**, which **one** of the following statements is correct?

Shade **one** circle only.

[1 mark]

A 7 in 10 people worldwide lack safely managed sanitation. ◯

B 4.5 billion people do not have access to safe, available water at home. ◯

C 6 in 10 people worldwide lack safely managed sanitation.

D 892 million people share a toilet or latrine with other households.

Evaluating sources

Some issue evaluation questions require an extended response and might ask you to draw on several different parts of a source. You should refer to the sources specifically and draw on your own knowledge.

Figure 2

Zuwera Abdul Latif, 22, lives in the village of Kakpayili-Shizugu in rural Ghana, where a new water kiosk is being built. Currently, Zuwera has to risk her health. "I go to the dam to fetch water. In a day I can go four times. The water is awful. It is green and you see insects in it." The new kiosk will sell water at a price that's affordable for the entire community. It will mean safer water closer to home for Zuwera and her young daughter. "I'm happy because when the water comes we will be cleaner every day," she says. "We will not fall sick. Everyone is happy about it."

 Worked example **Grades 5–9**

Two projects have been suggested to try to improve the access to safe water and sanitation for the rural poor in Ghana.

Project 1

A scheme funded by an NGO which will install a gravity fed water supply system in rural villages to provide them with a reliable supply of safe water. Local people will be involved in the project. They will help to build the pipeline and receive training so they can maintain it themselves.

Project 2

A large-scale project funded by the World Bank which will be implemented over the next five years. It will involve working with the government to improve the water supply and sanitation services throughout the country, beginning in urban areas.

Which of the projects do you think will improve the quality of life and socio-economic conditions for the rural poor in Ghana most effectively?

Use evidence from **Figure 1** (page 90) and **Figure 2**, as well as your own understanding, to explain why you have reached this decision. **[9 marks] [+ 3 SPaG marks]**

Both projects have the potential to improve the quality of life and socio-economic conditions for the rural poor in Ghana. Access to a secure supply of safe, clean water is important for improving socio-economic conditions, although as Figure 1 states, 2.3 billion people around the world still do not have basic sanitation services. Without them, people in rural areas can spend hours a day travelling to collect water, which may be contaminated. This increases their chances of catching waterborne diseases, which limit life expectancy. Safe water is also essential for economic development, as it is necessary for agriculture and industrial production...

Project 1 is likely to provide a reliable supply of water to the rural villages it reaches, as it involves technology which rural communities will be able to maintain themselves, ensuring access to safe water in the future. Villagers will also develop useful engineering skills, which may lead to further improvements for the whole community. Project 1 is also likely to have an immediate positive impact upon social conditions for women and children, as they are the people who would have had to travel long distances to collect water previously, as shown in Photograph A, and described in Figure 2...

In conclusion, project 1 would improve the quality of life and socio-economic conditions for the rural poor in Ghana more effectively than project 2. It would have immediate positive impacts on the health of the rural population, whereas project 2 would take longer to benefit the rural poor of Ghana...

In the exam, use all of the evidence from the resources booklet and your own understanding to support your answer to the 9 mark evaluative question.

In the conclusion, summarise the advantages and disadvantages of both projects. Choose one project only and clearly state why it is the most effective.

 Exam-style practice **Grades 5–9**

Project 2 would also improve the quality of life and socio-economic conditions for the rural poor in Ghana effectively. Use evidence from **Figure 1** on page 90, and **Figure 2**, as well as your own understanding to explain why. **[9 marks] [+ 3 SPaG marks]**

 **Made a start** **Feeling confident** 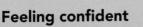 **Exam ready**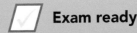

Making enquiries

As part of your GCSE Geography qualification, you will need to carry out **two** geographical enquiries, using data you have collected. You need to know how to formulate enquiry questions, carry out fieldwork based on physical and human processes, and analyse information and issues related to geographical enquiry.

 Enquiry questions and hypotheses

Before you carry out fieldwork, you need to choose an enquiry question and decide on a hypothesis to test. You need to know the geographical theory or concept that underpins your fieldwork as you could be asked about it in the exam.

Physical enquiry

An example of a physical enquiry question for rivers is:

How do the river characteristics along the River Dove change with distance downstream?

This question can be broken down into several hypotheses:

- The velocity of the River Dove increases with distance downstream.
- The cross-sectional area of the River Dove channel increases with distance downstream.

Human enquiry

An example of a human enquiry question for an urban study is:

Why are there variations in the quality of life in Manchester?

This question can be broken down into several hypotheses:

- Urban deprivation decreases as you move away from the central business district (CBD).
- The quality of the surrounding environment improves as you move away from the CBD.

 Six stage enquiries

1. **Identifying suitable questions for enquiry** – you must know the factors that need to be considered when selecting suitable questions for geographic enquiry, such as the relevance of your enquiry to the topics you have studied, and whether or not your hypotheses can be proven.

2. **Measuring and recording appropriate data** – when choosing data collection methods, you need to identify the potential risks of carrying out both human and physical fieldwork, and how these risks can be reduced.

3. **Selecting appropriate ways of processing and presenting fieldwork data** – you need to select appropriate methods for presenting your data and explain why you chose those methods.

4. **Describing, analysing and explaining fieldwork data** – you need to be able to use statistical techniques and identify anomalies in your data.

5. **Reaching conclusions** – you need to draw conclusions related to the original questions and aims of your enquiry.

6. **Evaluation of geographical enquiry** – you need to identify the limitations of your data and data collection methods, and evaluate the extent to which your conclusions were reliable.

 Exam focus

You will be assessed on your understanding of geographical enquiries in relation to:

- the use of fieldwork materials from an unfamiliar context
- your own enquiry work.

 Worked example   Grade 4

Figure 1 The River Kennet, Reading

Study **Figure 1**. Suggest one question or hypothesis that could be used for a river study.

[2 marks]

A hypothesis could be: The management techniques used along the River Kennet are successful at reducing the risk of flooding.

 Exam-style practice   Grade 4

For a physical enquiry on the topic of coastal landscapes, explain **one** possible risk of fieldwork and **one** way this risk could be reduced.

[4 marks]

Measuring and recording data

For both your physical and human enquiries, you need to understand how to measure and record fieldwork data using several different methods and be able to justify your data collection methods.

⑤ Key terms

- **Quantitative data** is numerical or fact-based. An example of a quantitative method would be measuring the width of a river in centimetres or metres.
- **Qualitative data** is non-numerical and opinion-based. An example of a qualitative method would be a questionnaire.
- **Primary data** is data that you collect yourself in the field. This might be done individually, in pairs or in small groups.
- **Secondary data** is data that has been obtained from another person or organisation. This type of data is important in generating background information for the study, which can help to support your own primary data.

⑤ Sampling methods

For each method, it is important that you decide where and how you will collect the data. It is not possible or practical for you to collect every possible relevant piece of data, so therefore a representative sample should be taken. There are three types of sampling:

1 **Random sampling** – collecting data at random, for example picking up stones from any part of a river bed.

2 **Systematic sampling** – collecting data at specific intervals, for example measuring the depth of the river at 30 cm intervals.

3 **Stratified sampling** – collecting data from different subsets of a parent population in order to obtain a fair representation of each group. The subsets have a known size. An example is collecting information from different age groups during a survey. Stratified sampling can be either random or systematic.

② Worked example — Grades 4–6

Figure 2 Students measuring the width of a river

Study **Figure 2**. State the type of data collected using this technique.

[1 mark]

Quantitative

Figure 1 A student conducting a questionnaire asking opinions to generate qualitative data

① Geographical skills

Each type of data has advantages and disadvantages. You need to know which type of data is best suited to your chosen enquiry. You could use more than one type of data in your enquiry.

⑤ Exam-style practice — Grades 4–6

For your human enquiry, explain **two** ways that you collected qualitative fieldwork data.

[4 marks]

Pages
**93,
101**

LINKS

Processing and presenting data

You need to know how to choose suitable presentation techniques to represent the data you have collected in your geographical enquiries, and how to interpret and analyse data presented in different ways.

 Types of data presentation

Depending on the study you complete, there are a range of presentation techniques that you can use. The following are suggestions of data presentation techniques that are appropriate for particular topics.

- **Rivers / coasts** – cross profiles, scattergraphs, maps showing proportional sediment size, bar charts, annotated field sketches of landforms or annotated photographs.
- **Urban issues and challenges** – land-use maps, divided bar charts, flow-line maps, choropleth maps or annotated photographs.

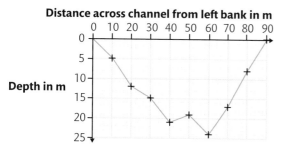

Figure 1 For a river study, this is a more complex presentation method to represent the cross-sectional area of the channel at different sites.

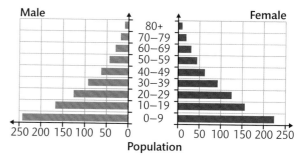

Figure 2 For an urban study, if you are investigating population change in a rural area, you could use a population pyramid.

 Worked example Grades 3–4

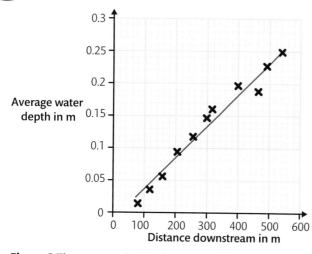

Figure 3 The average depth of water and distance downstream, Loughton Brook River

Study **Figure 3**.

(a) Draw a line of best fit.

[1 mark]

(b) Describe the relationship between average water depth and distance downstream.

[3 marks]

Figure 3 shows a positive correlation, which means that average water depth increases with distance downstream. At 120 m downstream the average water depth is 0.05 m, whereas at 520 m downstream the average water depth is 0.25 m.

Remember, when answering questions about graphs, maps and other visual data presentation methods, you need to support your points with specific data.

 Exam focus

In the exam, you could be asked to justify your choice of data presentation. Go to pages 101 and 102 to revise the advantages and disadvantages of the different presentation techniques.

 Exam-style practice Grades 4–5

For **one** of your data presentation techniques, explain **one** advantage and **one** disadvantage of using this technique to present your data.

[4 marks]

 Made a start **Feeling confident** **Exam ready**

Analysis, conclusion and evaluation

You need to know how to write a clear and focused analysis, how to draw your findings together to form a conclusion using evidence from your enquiry, and how to critically reflect on the reliability and validity of your fieldwork enquiries.

 5 Evaluating your enquiry

When evaluating your fieldwork enquiry, you need to reflect on the reliability of how you collected the data and the validity of your results and conclusions. This involves identifying limitations in the investigation, suggesting improvements, and discussing the reliability of your conclusion.

 Worked example   **Grade 6**

Analyse and conclude the results of your physical fieldwork investigation.

[6 marks]

The velocity of the River Dove increases from Site 1 to Site 6, with a mean velocity of 0.10 m/s at Site 1 compared with a mean velocity of 0.20 m/s at Site 6. This supports the Bradshaw Model, which states that the velocity of a river will increase downstream. One reason for this is that the increase in the river width and depth downstream means that there is proportionally less water in contact with the bed and banks, and thus less energy is lost due to friction.

The data includes an anomoly at Site 2, which could be the result of a measurement error. When the investigation was repeated, the data collected at Site 2 followed the expected trend.

In conclusion, the aim of my enquiry was to investigate how and why the river characteristics along the River Dove change with distance downstream. From the evidence I collected, I can conclude that the River Dove shows changes in its river characteristics that follow the Bradshaw Model. For example, the velocity of the river increased as we moved downstream from the source.

Exam focus

In the exam, you could be asked to evaluate one of your fieldwork enquiries, or you could be expected to evaluate fieldwork materials from an unfamiliar context.

Link primary and secondary data to the hypothesis.

Identify patterns and trends with reference to specific figures to support the points. Suggest reasons for the trend.

Discuss any data anomalies and offer possible explanations for their existence.

Summarise your findings in relation to the aim of the enquiry. State whether the hypothesis is proven or disproven based on the data.

Exam focus

There is a maximum of 3 marks available for:

- accurate spelling and punctuation
- correct grammar
- use of a range of relevant geographical terms.

SPaG marks are only awarded for 9-mark questions.

 10 Exam-style practice   **Grades 5–9**

For your physical environments enquiry, assess the reliability of the conclusions.

[9 marks] [+ 3 SpaG marks]

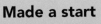

Map skills

Geographers use different types of maps to identify distributions and patterns of human and physical features. You need to know how to identify and describe different geographical features using maps at global, national and local scales.

⑤ Lines of latitude and longitude ✓

Lines of **latitude** and **longitude** are used to locate places accurately. Lines of latitude run horizontally around the Earth's surface from east to west. The key lines of latitude are: the equator (0°), Tropic of Cancer (23.5° north), Tropic of Capricorn (23.5° south), Arctic Circle (66.5° north), Antarctic Circle (66.5° south), North Pole (90° north) and the South Pole (90° south).

Lines of longitude run vertically, but unlike lines of latitude they meet at a point at the North and South poles. They are called **meridians**, and are measurements east or west of the Prime Meridian (also known as the Greenwich Meridian), which runs through Greenwich in London and is 0° longitude. The **International Date Line**, which separates calendar dates (when you cross it, the date changes), roughly follows 180° longitude.

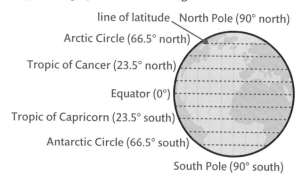
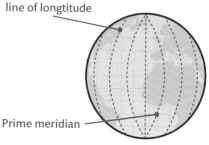

Figure 1 Lines of latitude and longitude

A **distribution** refers to the way geographical features are spread out or arranged.

A **pattern** is a way of showing a connection between geographical features.

When describing patterns of geographical features on a map you can use key terms like linear (along a line), dispersed (spread out) and nucleated (close together).

⑤ Worked example   Grades 4–5 ✓

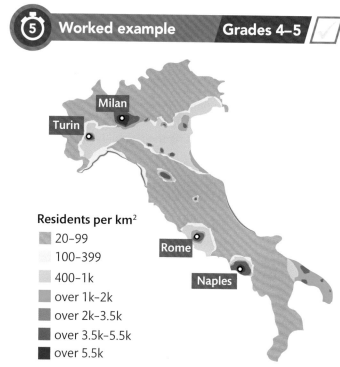

Residents per km²
- 20–99
- 100–399
- 400–1k
- over 1k–2k
- over 2k–3.5k
- over 3.5k–5.5k
- over 5.5k

Figure 2 Map of population density in Italy

Study **Figure 2**. Describe the distribution shown on the map.   **[3 marks]**

The map shows that the areas of highest population density are concentrated around the cities of Turin, Milan, Rome and Naples, all of which include areas of more than 3.5 thousand people per square kilometre. Generally, the areas of lowest population density are in the centre of the country, with large areas of 20-99 people per square kilometre, whilst there is higher population density in the north east of the country.

⑤ Exam-style practice   Grades 4–5 ✓

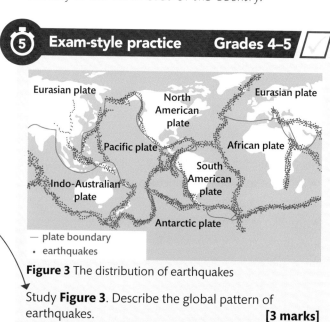

— plate boundary
• earthquakes

Figure 3 The distribution of earthquakes

Study **Figure 3**. Describe the global pattern of earthquakes.   **[3 marks]**

 Made a start   ✓ Feeling confident   ✓ Exam ready

Grid references and scale

You need to know how to use four- and six-figure grid references to find features on a map, be able to measure distances and understand scale.

⑤ Geographical skills

Using grid references

- To work out the **four-figure grid reference** of the shaded square, move east using the vertical lines (eastings) from the left edge of the map until you reach the left edge of the square. This is the first number, **33**. Then move from the bottom of the map northwards using the horizontal lines (northings) until you reach the bottom of the square. This is the second number, **81**. Therefore, the four-figure grid reference of the shaded square is **3381**.

- To work out the **six-figure grid reference** of the church with a tower, imagine that the grid squares are divided by lines into ten equal sections horizontally and vertically. Picturing the ten vertical lines, move east from the left edge of the square, **330**, to where the church symbol is, **335**. Then in the same way, move up from the bottom edge of the square, **810**, to the church at **815**. The six-figure grid reference for the church with a tower is **335815**.

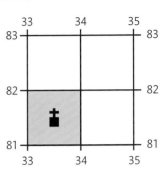

Figure 1 A simple grid

Measuring distances

For your exam, you could be asked to work out two types of distances using an OS map:

- **straight line distances,** such as a straight part of a road
- **curved line distances,** such as meanders along a river.

You will need a ruler to measure both types of distance, and a piece of string to measure curved line distances.

You will then need to convert the measurement using the **scale** on the map. The scale tells you how much smaller the area shown on the map is compared to the actual area. If you measure a road as 6 cm long on a map with the scale 1 : 50,000, the road is actually 3 km long, as 1 cm on the map is the equivalent to 500 m. However, if you measure a road as 6 cm long on a map with the scale 1 : 25,000, it means the road is 1.5 km long, as 1 cm on the map equals 250 m – a completely different answer.

② Worked example   Grade 7

1 What is located at reference 593244 on the map?

[2 marks]

Castle

2 What is the six-figure grid reference of the church near Bridstow?   **[2 marks]**

585249

3 Give the approximate curved-line distance (in km) from the public house to the roundabout along the A49.   **[1 mark]**

2 km

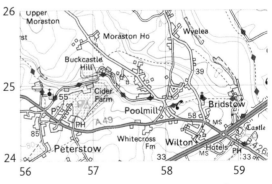

Figure 2 An OS map extract. Each of the grid squares is 2 cm by 2 cm, and the scale of the map is 1 : 50,000.

⑤ Exam-style practice   Grades 4–5

Study **Figure 2**.

(a) Give the four-figure grid reference for Whitecross farm.   **[1 mark]**

(b) Give the six-figure grid reference for the campsite south of Buckcastle Hill.   **[1 mark]**

(c) Give the straight-line distance (in km) from Poolmill to Wyelea.   **[1 mark]**

 Made a start   **Feeling confident**   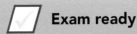 **Exam ready**

Pages
**31,
39, 48**
LINKS

Cross sections and contours

Geographers use cross sections to provide a visual representation of the relief and key features of a landscape. You need to know how to interpret a cross section and relate a cross-sectional drawing to relief features on a map.

5 OS maps features

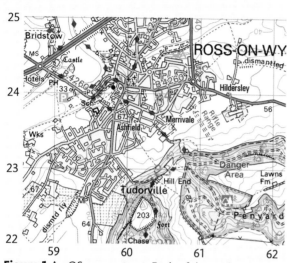

Figure 1 An OS map extract. Each of the grid squares is 2 cm by 2 cm, and the scale of the map is 1 : 50,000.

- **Contour lines** on maps indicate points of equal height above sea level. They are 10 m apart on 1 : 50,000 maps, and indicate the shape, size and height of key geographical features, such as river valleys and glacial landscape features.

- The distance between the contour lines represents **the gradient** of a slope. The closer the contour lines, the steeper the slope.

- You can identify **relief patterns** on a map by looking at contour lines. Lots of contour lines grouped closely together either side of more widely and evenly spaced contours tend to show a valley or spur.

- Black dots with a number represent **spot heights**. The number shows the height, in metres, above sea level.

5 Worked example　　Grade 2

1 Study **Figure 1**.

Give the six-figure grid reference of the triangulation pillar.　　**[1 mark]**

603224

2 What do contour lines show?

[2 marks]

Points of equal height above sea level

10 Drawing a cross section

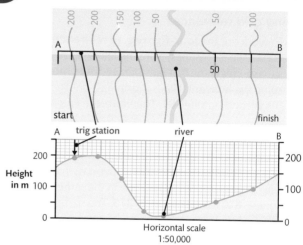

Figure 2 A cross section

1 Place a piece of paper along the chosen line.

2 Mark where the contour lines meet with the transect line and label the heights.

3 Mark on the location of key geographical features like rivers and roads.

4 Draw the axes for your graph, making the horizontal line the same length as the transect line.

5 Place your piece of paper over the horizontal line and mark each of the contour values on the graph with a cross.

6 Join up the crosses and label the location of any key features.

2 Exam focus

Remember, map skills can be tested in any of your exam papers. You also need to be able draw on your knowledge of coastal, fluvial and glacial landscapes to describe the features of these landscapes shown on a large-scale map.

Exam focus

For your exam, make sure you can confidently understand and use contours, road numbers, triangulation pillars and grid references.

2 Exam-style practice　　Grade 2

Study **Figure 1**. Give the height above sea level of the triangulation pillar.　　**[1 mark]**

Made a start　　**Feeling confident**　　**Exam ready**

Page
68
LINKS

Interpreting map features

OS maps can be used to interpret different physical and human features like settlement patterns, types of land use and communication networks. You need to know how to describe these features for your exam.

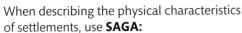

15 Interpreting maps

Settlement patterns
- a **dispersed** settlement is where buildings are spread out
- a **nucleated** settlement is where buildings are grouped
- a **linear** settlement is where buildings are built in a line.

When describing the physical characteristics of settlements, use **SAGA:**
Slope (gentle or steep)
Aspect (north, east, south or west facing)
Ground conditions (for example, floodplain)
Altitude (height above sea level)

Land use
You need to be able to recognise and describe types of land use. Make sure you're familiar with OS symbols, for example:

Coniferous trees  Non-coniferous woodland

Museum (recreational use) Castle or fort (historical/tourist site)

Industrial estate (land use)   Ind Est   Cattle grid (agricultural use)   CG

Transport networks
You need to be able to identify and describe roads, railway links, footpaths and cycle networks, for example:

Footpath   Traffic-free cycle route

Motorway   Road

For more on measuring length, go to page 97

Drainage

- A high density drainage system: impermeable land surface, lots of tributaries
- A low density drainage system: permeable land surface, fewer tributaries

Physical features
You need to be able to find and describe physical features of different landscapes on a map, for example:

Shingle   Vertical face/cliff

Flat rock   Slope

---

5 Worked example   Grade 8

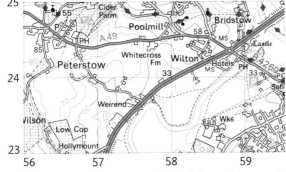

Figure 1 An OS map extract. Each of the grid squares is 2 cm by 2 cm, and the scale of the map is 1 : 50,000.

Other suitable answers are tributaries, small lakes and the hillside.

1 Study **Figure 1**. Identify one landscape feature shown in grid square 5723. **[1 mark]**

A meander in the river

2 Study **Figure 1**. Using evidence from the map, suggest whether it shows a mostly rural or mostly urban area. **[3 marks]**

The map shows a mostly rural area, because most of the map is empty land, settlement is dispersed and there are farms (Whitecross Farm). There is a small nucleated settlement (top left) but this suggests a village rather than a larger urban area.

---

2 Exam-style practice   Grade 4

Study **Figure 1**. Describe the shape of Wilton. **[2 marks]**

Using photos

BBC

You need to know how to interpret ground level, aerial and satellite photos and be able to draw and label sketches from photos.

(5) Three types of photographs

1 **Ground-level photos** are the most commonly used photos. They capture foreground detail like historical buildings and waterfalls.

2 **Aerial photos** are usually taken from helicopters or drones, looking down on the landscape. They can be **vertical** (looking directly down to the ground) or **oblique** (giving a more sideways view of the landscape).

3 **Satellite photos** are images of the surface of the Earth. They measure visible light, water vapour or infrared. Satellite images can be digitally enhanced to make features appear more prominent. They can be used to show vegetation or settlement patterns.

Figure 1 A satellite image of the Earth

(10) Drawing sketches

Figure 2 A photo of a meander

Figure 3 A sketch of the meander in **Figure 2**

In the exam, you could be asked to produce a sketch of, or label, a photograph, or label a map. When sketching from a photograph, focus on the key geographical features of the landscape and include anything that seems relevant to the question.

When you have completed your sketch you need to add labels and annotations. A **label** is a word or phrase that identifies key features, whereas an **annotation** is a description that provides additional details about an image. You need to be able to label and annotate both photographs and sketches.

> When you carry out fieldwork, sketching a map of the area can help you to remember the key features and layout of the landscape.

(1) Exam focus

For your exam, you may be asked, in combination with an OS map, to describe what geographical features a photograph shows or identify the direction in which a photograph was taken.

(5) Worked example   Grade 4

Suggest **one** benefit of using satellite photos.

[2 marks]

Satellite photos provide provide information from above, often over a wider area than normal photos. Scanners and sensors can be used to show vegetation and settlement patterns.

(5) Exam-style practice   Grade 3

Look carefully at **Figure 3**, the sketch of **Figure 2**. Suggest **one** label and **one** annotation.   **[3 marks]**

Made a start   Feeling confident   Exam ready

Graphs and charts

In the exam, you could be asked to complete or interpret different types of graphs. You need to know how to choose the most appropriate graph to represent different types of data.

(10) Types of graphs and charts

Line charts

A line chart represents continuous data that shows how something changes over time, such as population size. To accurately interpret a line chart, use a ruler to find the values on the x-axis and the y-axis.

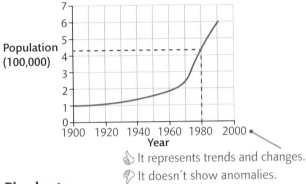

👍 It represents trends and changes.
👎 It doesn't show anomalies.

Pie charts

A pie chart represents proportions, such as a country's sources of energy.

If you are asked to complete a pie chart, you will need to find the angle of the segment. For instance, to work out the segment for coal, you need to find 20% of 360°.

$20 \div 100 = 0.2$
$0.2 \times 360° = 72°$

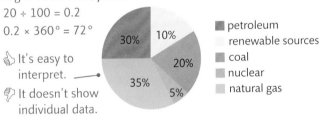

- petroleum
- renewable sources
- coal
- nuclear
- natural gas

👍 It's easy to interpret.
👎 It doesn't show individual data.

Pictograms

A pictogram represents data in a visual format with symbols. You read them in a similar way to a bar chart.

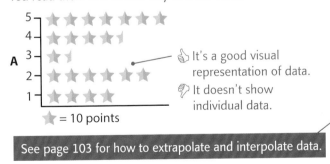

★ = 10 points

👍 It's a good visual representation of data.
👎 It doesn't show individual data.

See page 103 for how to extrapolate and interpolate data.

Bar charts

A bar chart represents discontinuous, generally numerical data that can be used to make comparisons, such as greenhouse gas emissions by country.

A divided bar chart can present multiple types of data.

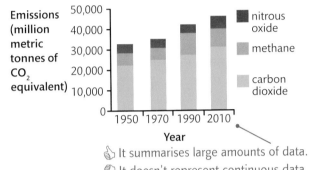

- nitrous oxide
- methane
- carbon dioxide

👍 It summarises large amounts of data.
👎 It doesn't represent continuous data.

Histograms

A histogram shows frequencies of groups of data, for instance the number of visitors that visit national parks each day.

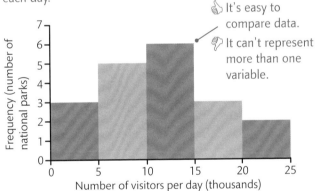

👍 It's easy to compare data.
👎 It can't represent more than one variable.

Scattergraphs

A scattergraph shows the relationship between two sets of data, such as rainfall and temperature. A **line of best fit** through the middle of the points is used to estimate other values.

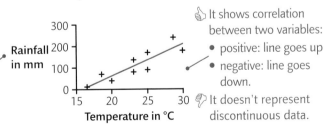

👍 It shows correlation between two variables:
- positive: line goes up
- negative: line goes down.

👎 It doesn't represent discontinuous data.

(5) Exam-style practice

1. Would a line graph or bar chart be most suitable for presenting a set of discontinuous data? **[1 mark]**
2. State whether the scattergraph above shows a positive or negative correlation. **[1 mark]**
3. State **two** types of graph that are suitable for presenting continuous data. **[2 marks]**

 Made a start   Feeling confident   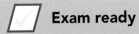 Exam ready

Maps and pyramids

In the exam, you could be asked to complete or interpret different types of maps or pyramids. You need to know the advantages and disavantages of each type.

 Types of maps and pyramids

Choropleth maps

A choropleth map represents data using different shades of colours. It is a useful way of showing how data, such as population density, can vary over a geographical area.

👍 It provides a good visual representation of data.

👎 It shows abrupt changes across boundaries.

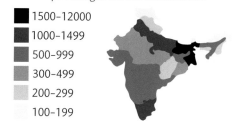

Dot maps

A dot map can represent distribution, or how a value changes between geographical areas, such as population density. In the map below, each dot represents the same number of people, so the more dots in a given area, the more people.

👍 It provides a good visual representation of data.

👎 Clusters of dots make it difficult to interpret data.

Isoline maps

An isoline map shows lines that link all the points on a map where there is an equal value to demonstrate a pattern over a large geographical area. They are often used to show data relating to weather. Contour lines, used to show relief and the shape of landforms, are a type of isoline.

👍 Changes can be easily identified.

👎 It requires large amounts of data.

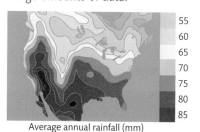

Average annual rainfall (mm)

Population pyramids

A population pyramid shows an overview of an area's population characteristics, such as gender and age group.

👍 The general shape can provide quick access to data trends.

👎 Some detail is lost in data groups.

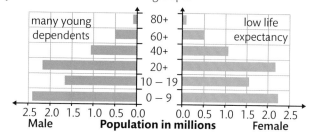

Flow-line maps

A flow-line map uses arrows to represent the size of a variable and the direction of movement, often the movement of people and goods between areas or countries.

👍 The scale and width of lines can be used to add extra detail.

👎 Distance and direction may not be represented accurately.

Proportional symbols maps

A proportional symbols map uses different sized shapes to represent data.

👍 It's a good way of representing changing values.

👎 It can be difficult to produce.

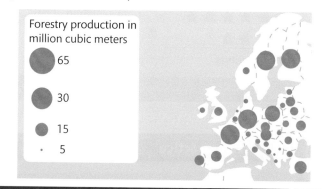

Forestry production in million cubic meters

65

30

15

5

 Exam-style practice **Grades 2–4**

Study the population pyramid. What was the total population for the 10–19 age group? **[1 mark]**

 Made a start **Feeling confident** 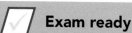 **Exam ready**

Statistical skills

In the exam, you could be expected to use appropriate measures of central tendency and spread, calculate percentage increase and decrease, and interpolate and extrapolate trends in data.

 Measures of central tendency

Measures of central tendency are also known as averages.

Calculating averages

- **Mean** – add all the values together and divide by the number of values. The mean can be affected by extreme values.

- **Median** – organise the values numerically from lowest to highest and take the middle value. If there are two middle values, the median is halfway between them. The median is not affected by extreme values.

- **Mode** – find the value that occurs most often. This can apply to data that are not numerical, such as colours.

- **Modal class** – if the data set is grouped into classes, find the class with the highest frequency.

 Measures of spread

Measures of spread show how the data are distributed, for instance the **interquartile range** shows how far values are spread from the median.

The **range** is calculated by subtracting the smallest value from the largest value. If the range is big, the spread of the data is large. Spread can be affected by extreme values.

To find the interquartile range you must work out the upper and lower quartiles. The IQR is the difference between these two values. The median is the central value of the IQR.

Lower quartile = $\frac{1}{4}(n + 1)$th value

n is the number of values in the data set.

Upper quartile = $\frac{3}{4}(n + 1)$th value

IQR = upper quartile – lower quartile

 Worked example   Grade 4

1 Find the interquartile range of this set of numbers.   **[2 marks]**

1 12 15 19 20 24 28 34 37 47 50

Lower quartile = $\frac{1}{4}(11 + 1)$ = 3rd value so the lower quartile is 15

Upper quartile = $\frac{3}{4}(11 + 1)$ = 9th value so the upper quartile is 37

Interquartile range = 37 – 15 = 22.

2 The number of shoppers that visited a supermarket in January was 8000 and in February was 14,000. Calculate the percentage increase.   **[2 marks]**

14,000 − 8000 = 6000

6000 ÷ 8000 = 0.75

0.75 × 100 = 75%

To work out a percentage increase or decrease, find the difference between the two numbers you are comparing, divide this number by the original number and multiply the answer by 100. For a percentage decrease, the answer will be a negative number.

 Interpolating and extrapolating trends

Interpolating and extrapolating trends in a data set allows you to predict a value that you don't have any data for.

- Interpolation is estimating an unknown value within a data set.
- Extrapolation is estimating an unknown value outside a data set.

You can estimate an unknown value by plotting the data you do have on a graph, and then using the line of best fit to predict the unknown value. To extrapolate, extend the line of best fit beyond the first and last point. You can estimate the values by reading from the line of best fit. See page 101 for information on scattergraphs and lines of best fit.

Interpolation and extrapolation is particularly useful for predicting environmental conditions, such as rainfall, temperature or air pollution levels, at locations for which you have no data.

 Exam-style practice   Grade 4

The UK's population increased from approximately 55 million in 1970 to approximately 62 million in 2010. What is the percentage increase?   **[1 mark]**

 Made a start   **Feeling confident**   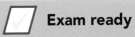 **Exam ready**

Answers

Page 1 Defining natural hazards

Changing climatic conditions, like a rise in temperatures, can increase the frequency of droughts. Rising ocean temperatures caused by climate change also affect natural hazard risk, as they increase the frequency and severity of storm surges, flooding and tropical storms. Another factor is urbanisation; an increasing proportion of the global population live in urban areas, leading to more people living in densely populated areas at risk of flooding.

Page 2 Distribution of earthquakes and volcanoes

The majority of volcanoes occur on or near plate boundaries. The areas with the highest concentration of volcanoes are around the Pacific plate, which is known as the 'Ring of Fire', and along the boundary between the South American and Nazca plates, which has resulted in a linear pattern of volcanoes on the western coast of South America. However, there are some volcanoes that occur away from plate boundaries, like those in the middle of the Eurasian plate.

Page 3 Plate margin activity

At constructive plate margins convection currents cause two tectonic plates to move away from each other. As the plates separate magma rises up to the surface, forming a volcano.

Page 4 Earthquake effects

This question is marked for SPaG (spelling, punctuation and grammar).

The effects of earthquakes vary considerably between HICs and LICs. Generally, primary effects of earthquakes in LICs tend to be far more severe; they tend to cause greater numbers of fatalities and casualties than earthquakes which occur in wealthier countries. The difference between earthquake effects is shown by the examples of Nepal's 2015 earthquake and Ecuador's 2016 earthquake. Despite the fact that both earthquakes were of the same magnitude – 7.8 on the Richter scale – in Nepal, over 8000 people were killed and many thousands more were injured, whereas only 650 people were killed by the earthquake in Ecuador. As well as resulting in higher numbers of fatalities, the effect of earthquakes upon buildings and infrastructure also tends to be more severe in an LIC. This is illustrated by these examples. Whilst the earthquake in Ecuador destroyed or damaged more than 7000 buildings and caused around 26,000 people to be displaced, more than 600,000 buildings in the Nepalese capital of Kathmandu and nearby towns were damaged or destroyed, which left approximately 2.8 million people homeless after the earthquake.

The vast difference in the effects of the two earthquakes is largely due to the fact that wealthier countries can afford better seismic monitoring systems, so they can make predictions and give warnings. HICs can also afford to construct buildings which are designed to withstand earthquakes. LICs cannot afford to invest in infrastructure, and houses may be built out of scrap materials like wood and corrugated iron, which are more likely to be destroyed in an earthquake. To conclude, as the examples of the recent earthquakes in Nepal and Ecuador show, the effects of earthquakes in an LIC are much more severe than in a wealthier country, often because of a lack of planning and protection strategies in LICs.

Page 5 Earthquake responses

NGOs, like Oxfam, provide vital assistance to countries responding to a tectonic hazard, and can play an important part in a country's long-term response. For example, following the Ecuadorian earthquake in 2016, Oxfam worked with local communities to educate people on basic hygiene practices to reduce the spread of waterborne diseases. Oxfam also worked with the government to rebuild water supply systems.

Page 6 Living with natural hazards

One economic reason why people choose to live in volcanically active areas is that they generally have very fertile soils because of the minerals found in volcanic ash. Fertile soil increases crop yields for farmers. *You could also have mentioned geothermal energy or tourism.*

Page 7 Reducing the risk

Protection methods can be used to reduce the effects of earthquakes on both people and buildings. One protection method is designing and building earthquake-proof buildings which can be constructed to withstand the tremors. For example, buildings can be fitted with shock absorbers and counterweights to help absorb the shockwaves and keep the buildings upright. This reduces the number of buildings destroyed and the number of people killed by collapsing buildings when an earthquake occurs. A planning method that effectively reduces the fatal effects of earthquakes is planning and practising evacuation, which helps people to escape quickly and safely. *You could also have mentioned earth embankments or exclusion zones.*

Page 8 General atmospheric circulation model

Solar radiation causes hot dry conditions at the equator and rising air. This produces low pressure. The air moves north and south, and cools and sinks at latitudes of 30°. The cooled air moves back towards the equator, which is known as the trade winds, whilst the rest of the air moves towards the poles, forming part of the Ferrel cells.

The trade winds cause distinctive climate patterns; they gather moisture which can result in rainfall when they blow over land in tropical regions.

Where the warmer air of the Ferrel cells meets the cool dry air from the Polar cells at about 60°, the polar jet stream is formed. Northwards and southwards of 60° latitude, cold polar air circulates in the Polar cells, with prevailing polar easterly winds that cause cold dry weather conditions.

Page 9 Distribution of tropical storms

One factor that influences the distribution of tropical storms is sea temperature, as tropical storms can only form in areas where the temperature is at least 26.5 °C at the sea's surface. *You could also have mentioned: latitude (between approximately 5° and 30° latitude), the amount of water vapour in the atmosphere; the location of areas of low pressure and storms joining; or the Coriolis effect.*

Page 10 Causes and features of tropical storms

Tropical storms are formed where surface water temperatures are at least 26.5 °C. The warm ocean leads to rapidly rising warm air and water evaporating, which causes thunderstorms. Where these storms converge, a zone of very low pressure is created. As the air rises it starts to spin, accelerating in speed. The rising air cools and condenses, creating cumulonimbus clouds, which leads to heavy rainfall, thunder and lightning. The Coriolis effect causes the storm to spiral around the central calmer point, known as the eye.

Page 11 Typhoon Haiyan

This is an example of how to structure a named example response. You should use the named example you have studied in class.

Typhoon Haiyan, a Category 5 hurricane, started in the western Pacific Ocean on 2nd November 2013 and moved over the Philippines, affecting more than 14 million people. One of the immediate responses to the tropical storm was that the Canadian and UK governments sent shelter kits for families to make emergency shelters or temporarily repair their homes. Over 1.4 million buildings were damaged or destroyed, so other immediate responses included evacuation centres being established to provide shelter for people who had been made homeless. Other countries, such as the USA and Japan, also supplied water and household items to help people whose homes had been destroyed to cope with day-to-day life. Long-term responses to a tropical storm may include repairing buildings and reconstructing essential infrastructure such as roads and electricity supply systems. For example, the long-term response to Typhoon Haiyan included Philippine Red Cross volunteers helping to rebuild people's homes. Many of the new homes were strategically built away from the potential flood risk areas to reduce damage from future tropical storms. Another long-term response to Typhoon Haiyan by the Red Cross was working with people to educate them on disaster planning and developing strategies to reduce the risks caused by future tropical storms.

Page 12 Planning for tropical storms

One way that countries can plan for tropical storms is the installation of early warning systems, such as the one in Bangladesh, which allow time for people to evacuate. They help to reduce the death toll. *You could also have mentioned: using information from the Red Cross or stocking up on food and water.*

Page 13 Weather in the UK

One type of weather hazard experienced in the UK is heavy rainfall over a long period, which can lead to major flooding. *You could also have mentioned: snow; very cold conditions; heatwaves; flash floods; and storms.*

Page 14 UK extreme weather events

One of the strategies that could be used to reduce the risk of flooding in the UK is dredging rivers regularly to increase the carrying capacity of river channels. For example, the River Tone and the River Parrett in Somerset have been dredged following the flood in 2014. This allows rivers to carry a greater volume of water, which increases the time it takes before rivers burst their banks and flood. Another management strategy that could be used is to repair existing flood defences and build new tidal barriers in strategic positions. In Somerset, planning has begun for a new tidal barrier on the River Parrett. Temporary pumping sites in Somerset have now been made permanent to enable water to drain quickly throughout the year. *You could also have mentioned: raising road levels.*

Page 15 Climate change evidence

Evidence of climate change includes a rise in global sea levels. In the 20th century, global sea levels rose by about 14 cm, and are rising faster now than they were 50 years ago. There has also been a decrease in snow cover in locations across the northern hemisphere. For example, scientists recorded record low levels of snow in North America three times between 2008 and 2012. Other evidence for climate change includes temperature records; 2010 was the warmest year globally since records began. Ice cores provide evidence for climate change, as they contain bubbles of air from when the ice was formed, so scientists can analyse ice cores to determine the climate at the time the ice was formed. This method has shown that there have been significant changes in the Earth's climate over millions of years. *You could also have mentioned: thickness of sea ice; glaciers retreating; coral reefs bleaching; or decrease in size of ice sheets.*

Page 16 Causes of climate change

One human cause of climate change is increased rates of deforestation. This leads to a rise in carbon dioxide (a greenhouse gas) in the atmosphere, which contributes to global warming. *You could also have mentioned: burning fossil fuels; agriculture; or beef production.*

Page 17 Managing climate change

One way humans have adapted to climate change is by building houses on stilts, especially on low-lying islands such as the Maldives. Building houses above water level means that the risk of potential flooding is reduced. *You could also have mentioned: changing agricultural methods (irrigation, genetics); or managing water use to make supply more sustainable.*

Page 18 Using examples and case studies

When comparing the effectiveness of the immediate and long-term responses to earthquakes or volcanic eruptions, discuss the similarities and differences between the two examples you have chosen. Make sure you include specific information about at least two immediate responses and two long-term responses.

Page 19 A small-scale ecosystem

If the population of herbivores in a small-scale ecosystem rapidly decreased, it may cause the population of carnivores to also decrease. For example, in Frensham Little Pond, if the population of herbivores, such as pond snails, rapidly decreased then the population of carnivores, such as ducks, which rely on them as a source of food, is also likely to decrease as there would no longer be enough food to support the existing carnivore population.

Page 20 Tropical rainforests

Tropical rainforests are mostly located between the Tropic of Cancer and the Tropic of Capricorn. The largest areas of tropical rainforest are in Central and South America, Indonesia and West and Central Africa. There are also some smaller areas of rainforest existing outside the tropics, such as some of the isolated areas of rainforest in Asia.

Page 21 Deforestation in Indonesia

Indonesia has one of the highest rates of deforestation in the world. Deforestation has destroyed millions of hectares of rainforest across the archipelago, causing severe loss of habitat for the thousands of species living there. The felling of trees has caused soil erosion, as there are no trees to protect the soil from the heavy rain, which leads to greater surface run-off and flooding. Carbon dioxide has been released by felling and burning trees, increasing greenhouse gas emissions. Deforestation has contributed to Indonesia becoming one of the world's biggest emitters of greenhouse gases. Deforestation has also helped to facilitate an increase in mining activities, and local people have often been exploited, having to work in dangerous conditions on low wages. There have been violent conflicts between locals and private companies over the use of the land. However, the new mines have meant that the country has been able to produce valuable exports, such as gold, copper and palm oil, which have helped develop the economy. Indonesia is now the sixteenth largest economy in the world.

Page 22 Sustainable rainforests

One of the ways tropical rainforests can be managed sustainably is by replanting trees to re-establish wildlife habitats that have been damaged through destructive human activities, like palm oil production. Another management strategy involves governments working in collaboration with NGOs, like the WWF, to prevent illegal logging and promote the sustainable trade of legal timber. This can help a country's economy benefit from the rainforest without increasing deforestation. Another strategy involves managing tourism in tropical rainforests by using soft trekking, which directs tourists through specifically designed trails and helps to protect wildlife and plant species. Finally, managing rainforests sustainably also involves tackling the causes of deforestation, such as local people cutting down trees to clear land for subsistence farming. Working with local communities to ensure they can make a living from the rainforest, such as through producing Brazil nuts, gives them an incentive to protect it.

Page 23 Characteristics of hot deserts

1. Answers could include: they receive low amounts of annual rainfall, averaging less than 250 mm per year; or they have a hot and dry climate – temperatures can reach more than 50 °C.

2. Hot deserts are generally located between 30 °N and 30 °S of the equator. The largest areas of desert are in Africa and the Middle East. For example, the Sahara Desert stretches across North Africa. There are also some deserts which are located further north and south, such as the Patagonian desert in South America.

Page 24 Opportunities and challenges in a hot desert

One of the opportunities provided by hot deserts is tourism, which provides employment and helps the economy. Tourist attractions include activities like camel trekking and 4x4 rides, such as at Erg Chebbi in Morocco. These activities create jobs for locals to act as tour guides, improving their quality of life by giving them an income. A second opportunity provided by these landscapes is the availability and extraction of valuable fossil fuel reserves like oil. For example, the oil and gas sector is vital for the economy of countries like Algeria, where it accounts for 35 per cent of total gross domestic product. The income generated by the trading of this resource can be used to improve the infrastructure of the whole country and help it to develop. A challenge created by hot desert environments is the extreme temperatures. For example, the Sahara Desert is one of the driest places on Earth with a mean yearly temperature of 30 °C, and temperatures reaching up to 50 °C during the summer. These extreme temperatures can cause health risks, such as dehydration. Another related challenge in hot desert environments is drought, due to the heat and the lack of rainwater.

Page 25 Desertification

One way the rate of desertification can be reduced is through planting trees. This means that soil erosion is reduced because the tree roots stabilise the structure of the soil. A second way of reducing desertification is through the use of appropriate technology, such as using rocks to create a wall around farmers' fields. This means that water is trapped, which maintains soil moisture and increases crop production, and helps to prevent desertification.

Page 26 Characteristics of cold environments

1. Answers could include: it has an average winter temperature of about –34 °C; it has a soil layer frozen for most of the year; or it is home to animals such as wolves, musk oxen and Arctic foxes.

2. Answers could include: plants have adapted to cold environments by growing close to the ground to reduce potential damage from the wind and ice, for example the snow saxifrage; or plants have adapted to cold environments by growing quickly in spring when temperatures rise.

Page 27 Opportunities and challenges in tundra

One of the challenges for people when trying to develop cold environments is the extreme temperatures, which can be as low as –60 °C in winter. This poses a serious risk of hypothermia, which can cause death, and means that thermal clothing and footwear are necessary for anyone living or working there. A second challenge is the remoteness of many cold environments. Many parts of them are hard to reach and have very limited transport links. Heavy snow in cold environments can also limit the types of transport which can be used. This can make it difficult to transport heavy construction materials and machinery.

Page 28 Conservation of cold environments

One approach to managing cold environments is through the establishment of international agreements like The Antarctic Treaty, which was signed by 12 countries in 1959 to ensure that human activities are regulated and monitored in order to preserve the landscape. Another stakeholder managing cold environments is the World Wildlife Fund, a global conservation group. Through its Arctic Programme, the WWF works to ensure that the use of resources is sustainable, as well as raising awareness by educating people about the importance of protecting the landscape.

Page 29 Landscapes in the UK

Figure 1 shows that most upland landscapes in the UK are in the north and west. The largest areas of high land, between 400 and 800 metres above sea level and some very high areas over 800 metres above sea level, are located in central and north Scotland. Most of the islands off the north-west coast of the UK are upland landscapes too; most of the land is between 150 and 399 metres above sea level. **Figure 1** also shows that much of Wales, in the west of the UK, is an upland landscape, as large areas of the country are at least 400 metres above sea level. However, there are also some upland landscapes in the south of the UK too, mainly in the south west. There are no upland landscapes in the south east or east midlands of the UK, the majority of which is less than 149 metres above sea level.

Page 30 Waves and weathering

1. Any one from: constructive waves have a long wavelength; they generally occur up to nine times per minute; they have a low wave height; they have a strong swash and weak backwash; or they cause deposition of material.

2. Rain enters cracks in the rock and freezes, which expands the cracks and puts pressure on the rock. When repeated over time, freezing and thawing weakens the rocks and eventually breaks them down.

Page 31 Coastal erosion landforms

1. An arch, such as Durdle Door in Dorset, forms from erosion taking place on a headland. The prevailing winds blow destructive waves towards the base of a headland. Processes of erosion, such as hydraulic power (the force of the waves compressing the air in the cracks between rocks), exploit faults, which are cracks or areas of weakness in the headland. Over time, the faults increase in size and eventually become a small cave. Continued erosional processes like hydraulic action and abrasion (the collision of rock fragments with the face of the cliff), cause the cave to deepen. If two caves form either side of a headland, erosion will eventually cause the backs of the caves to break through, forming an arch.

2. One erosional process involved in shaping a wave cut platform is abrasion. It is the action of small pieces of rock, carried in seawater, being hurled against a cliff by waves and causing pieces of the cliff to chip off. Abrasion shapes a wave cut platform by contributing to the formation of a wave cut notch, which is when pieces of the cliff are eroded until a cliff overhang is formed. Eventually, the overhang collapses, forming a wave cut platform. Over time, erosion smooths the exposed rock of the wave cut platform.

Page 32 Mass movement and transportation

1. Any one from: sliding (the sudden movement of large volumes of material along an area of saturated soil); slumping (the mass movement of saturated permeable rock and soil on top of impermeable rock); or rock falls (the free-fall movement of rock fragments due to gravity).

2. Slumping can result in large sections of cliffs collapsing onto the beach below; the loss of farmland and coastal properties; and the destruction of stretches of coastal footpaths.

Page 33 Coastal deposition landforms

1. (1) The formation of a spit, such as Spurn Head, starts with prevailing winds causing the swash of the waves to push sediment onto the beach at an angle.
(2) The backwash will then bring much of the material back down the beach at right angles to the coast, under the force of gravity.
(3) The swash and backwash process will result in a zig zag movement of material along the coastline, known as longshore drift.
(4) When there is a sudden change in the direction of the coastline, longshore drift continues to transport the material in the same direction as before rather than following the changing shape of the coastline, and the transported material is deposited offshore.
(5) Over time deposited material continues to accumulate until a spit forms, stretching across from the headland. The spit becomes curved towards its end due to the direction of strong secondary winds.
(6) As the spit grows, sheltered waters develop behind it. This causes finer sediments to settle and begin to fill in the area, eventually leading to the development of a salt marsh.

2. Low-energy constructive waves

Page 34 Hard engineering

(a) Rock armour or riprap

(b) Either of these advantages: it is relatively cheap and helps to absorb wave energy; or it is quick to implement. Either of these disadvantages: it is unattractive; or it can become damaged during heavy storms.

Page 35 Soft engineering

1. One reason why a managed retreat policy might be adopted along a stretch of coastline is if the value of the land is deemed low, such as farmland. Installing hard engineering strategies to manage erosion can be extremely costly, so it is cheaper to provide compensation to the farmer than to install and maintain expensive engineering methods. A second reason for adopting this policy is that it encourages the formation of habitats such as salt marshes. The flooding of Northey Island in Essex (in 1991) is an example of a managed retreat scheme. These are important for encouraging biodiversity in the local area.

2. Any one of: sand dune regeneration helps to protect the coastline because sand dunes form a physical barrier between the sea and the coastline, and they can absorb wave energy, helping to reduce erosion.

Page 36 Coastal management

Man-made changes to the coastal environment can have significant positive and negative effects upon conservation strategies. The implementation of hard engineering management strategies can effectively reduce erosion along a stretch of coastline, which can help to protect areas which are a conservation priority. For example, at Walton-on-the-Naze in Essex, many man-made changes have been made, including installing a sea wall and rock armour. Although these change the appearance of the coastal environment, they help to protect the Naze tower, a site of historical value, and a nature reserve and SSSI area from the fast rate of erosion along that stretch of coastline. However, man-made changes can also adversely affect conservation in coastal environments. Development in coastal areas popular with tourists can result in land being built on which some people may wish to conserve as areas for wildlife, such as wading birds.

Page 37 A river profile

C a stream that joins the main river

Page 38 Fluvial processes

1. Any one from: traction, suspension, solution or saltation.

2. Hydraulic action and abrasion increase both the width and depth of the river channel as the water moves downstream. Hydraulic action is the sheer force of the water hitting the bed and banks of a river, and trapping air in cracks. The increasing pressure weakens the bed and banks and wears them away, widening and deepening the river channel. Abrasion is the action of rock fragments carried by the river scraping against the banks and bed of the river channel, which causes them to wear down. Both processes increase the cross-sectional area of the river.

Page 39 Fluvial erosion landforms

The cycle of less resistant rock being eroded by the hydraulic action and abrasion of a waterfall will lead to the collapse of unsupported, more resistant rock. As a waterfall retreats upstream, for example downstream of Niagara Falls, this repeated cycle will form a steep-sided gorge.

Page 40 Fluvial erosion and deposition landforms

Both erosional and depositional processes are involved in the formation of meanders. Meanders are generally found in the middle section of a river, e.g. River Severn, because lateral erosion is common there. On the outside bend of a meander, the current is moving quickly, so the force of the water against the bed and the banks begins to wear them away; this is an erosional process known as hydraulic action. On the opposite side, on the inside of the bend, sand and shingle are deposited, as the flow is slower and friction is at its greatest. Over time this forms what is known as a slip-off slope. With erosion on the outer bend and deposition on the inner bend, the meanders begin to migrate, shifting position from side to side and moving downstream.

Page 41 Flood risk

1. One of the physical factors that causes an increase in the risk of flooding is geology. If the area surrounding the river channel is formed from impermeable rock, the water will not be able to infiltrate. This will increase surface run-off, leading to the water reaching the river channel at a much faster rate, and increase the risk of flooding. A second physical factor which increases the risk of flooding is the gradient of the slopes. If there are steep slopes surrounding the river channel, this will cause the water to run across the ground at a much faster rate, leading to the water reaching the channel much more quickly than if the slopes had a gentler gradient.

2. One of the potential economic impacts for the town of Mytholmroyd following the flood is the loss of income for any local businesses, both because people may be unable to access them during the flood, and because businesses may need to temporarily close for repairs once the flood waters recede. A potential social impact of the flooding for the village is damage to people's homes which could make them uninhabitable and lead to temporary homelessness. This is likely to be very distressing for the people involved and make it very difficult for them to rebuild their lives. This could lead to another economic impact, the cost of repairing flood damage in the town, which could be very expensive.

Page 42 Flood hydrographs

1. 6 hours

2. Heavy precipitation may lead to a higher peak discharge on a flood hydrograph because it is likely to result in land becoming saturated quickly and more water reaching the river, which contributes to the volume of water in the river. Lighter, intermittent periods of precipitation can cause a longer lag time on a flood hydrograph because this type of precipitation is more likely to infiltrate into the soil, reducing surface run-off, so the time it takes the water to reach the channel will be longer.

Page 43 Hard engineering

Either of these advantages: they can provide an additional source of water not just to the surrounding area but further afield too; they can be used for hydroelectric power. Either of these disadvantages: they are very expensive to install and maintain; they can cause farmland downstream to be less fertile.

Page 44 Soft engineering

C Restoring the river to its natural course is not a guaranteed protection against flooding downstream.

Page 45 Flood management

In Boscastle, a £10 million flood management scheme was installed to protect the community. One of the reasons for installing the flood management scheme was the devastation caused by the 2004 floods. Immediate economic impacts of the flood included damage to 58 properties, and more than 100 cars being swept away. Installing the flood management scheme helped reduce the risk of similar issues caused by flooding happening again. *Other reasons you could include are the damage to local properties, other businesses and the danger to people's lives.*

Page 46 Glacial processes

1. Rotational slip occurs when the glacier becomes lubricated during the summer by melted water, causing it to slide downhill, transporting material within it. *You could also describe bulldozing instead.*

2. Plucking is the action of the glacier removing parts of the bedrock, as they become attached to the glacier by freezing and are pulled out when the glacier moves. Abrasion occurs when the bottom of a glacier rubs against bedrock, leaving behind a smooth surface with scratches in it, called striations.

Page 47 Glacial erosion landforms

1. An arête, such as Striding Edge in the Lake District, is formed from the erosional processes acting on two back-to-back corries, creating a long knife-edged ridge between them.

2. A glacial trough is formed when a glacier cuts through a V-shaped river valley. The processes of abrasion and plucking erode the sides and bottom of the valley, creating a wider, flat-bottomed glacial trough.

Page 48 Glacial transportation and deposition landforms

A drumlin is a small elongated hill with a steeper blunt end and a smooth tapered end. The steeper blunt end faces the direction the glacial ice is coming from. The long axis of the drumlin helps scientists to ascertain the direction the glacier moved in.

Page 49 Economic activities

Farming can provide economic opportunities in glaciated upland landscapes, such as Snowdonia, as the thin infertile soils, steep slopes, and short growing season in glaciated upland landscapes provide ideal grazing areas for sheep. Forestry also provides opportunities in upland glacial landscapes, as the soils are suitable for the growing of conifer trees. This creates employment in glaciated upland areas, boosting the economy.

Page 50 Tourism in Snowdonia

1. One environmental impact of tourism on glaciated environments is disturbance of, and damage to, wildlife habitats caused by tourists dropping litter.

2. One way tourism can be sustainably managed in glaciated environments like Snowdonia is the creation of designated walkways, preventing tourists from entering the more fragile areas, which limits further damage. A second management strategy is educating tourists about the importance of protecting the landscape using information boards.

Page 51 Levelled response questions

Spits like the one shown in **Figure 2** and at Spurn Head form where the prevailing wind blows at an angle to the coastline, resulting in longshore drift.

Where the shape of the coastline changes, often at the mouth of an estuary, sediment is deposited, and accumulates to form a spit over time. Strong secondary winds cause the end of the spit to curve.

Page 52 Urbanisation characteristics

One push factor affecting urbanisation is a lack of well-paid employment opportunities in remote rural areas.

One pull factor is access to good medical facilities. *You could also have mentioned: entertainment or transport.*

Page 53 Expanding Mumbai: opportunities

Answers could include any two of the following: educational opportunities, as there are more than 1000 primary and secondary schools in Mumbai; better-paid employment prospects; a wider range of employment prospects, as Mumbai has a growing manufacturing sector and there is also a high demand for services, such as couriers and cleaners.

Page 54 Expanding Mumbai: challenges

Mumbai is located in India, a newly emerging economy. It is one of the most densely populated cities in the world and rapid urban growth has created a number of challenges. One of these challenges is providing access to clean water and sanitation systems for the rapidly expanding population. There is limited access to clean water, with the use of standpipes restricted to first thing in the morning for two hours for hundreds of families. This means that those who haven't got access to the standpipes are forced to use water from streams and rivers, and as only 60% of households are connected to Mumbai's sewerage system, these waterways are often polluted. This can lead to the spread of waterborne diseases.

Other challenges created by Mumbai's rapid growth include congestion in the city's transport system. The rapid influx of people migrating to the city has led to an increase in the number of cars, with an estimated 2 million on Mumbai's roads. This has led to a rise in traffic congestion and air pollution. Finally, rapid urban growth has put increasing pressure on key services like healthcare and education. In Dharavi, there is a significant strain on the Sion Hospital. This means that many people have to wait a long time to be treated.

Page 55 Distribution of UK population and cities

Figure 1 shows that the main pattern of population density is that high population densities tend to be concentrated in major cities, and that the area with the highest population density is the south-east of the UK. The capital city of London has the highest population density, up to 14,500 people per square km, and the Scottish and Northern Irish capitals of Edinburgh and Belfast respectively also have high population densities. The largest areas of very low population density are in Scotland, in particular the Scottish Highlands and Islands.

Page 56 Expanding London: Opportunities

The location of the city of London creates both social and economic opportunities. It is located in the south-east of the UK near to a number of large airports, such as Heathrow, and is in a central location in terms of time-zone. This makes it an ideal base for business people travelling regularly to the east and west, which helps London to attract highly skilled workers from around the world. Its location has also contributed to social opportunities in the city; it is a very popular destination for international migrants to the UK, who have made London one of the most culturally diverse places in the country.

Page 57 Expanding London: Challenges

The Lower Lea Valley Urban Redevelopment Project, in East London, helped to regenerate a deprived part of East London. One reason the area needed regeneration was that it suffered from high rates of unemployment. The new 500-acre Olympic Park created employment opportunities both during and after construction. A second reason that regeneration was needed was that the area consisted of derelict industrial buildings. To address this problem, the redevelopment included building 9000 new homes to regenerate the area.

Page 58 Urban sustainability

For sustainable urban living, it is necessary to carefully manage resources and transport systems.

Rising affluence is leading to increased car ownership in cities in both LICs and HICs. However, using cars as the main mode of transport in densely populated areas is not sustainable, as it increases traffic congestion and can lead to increased levels of air pollution, which may result in respiratory problems. To create sustainable urban living, car use should be restricted and alternative transport systems which are affordable, low-carbon and less polluting should be promoted. For example, in Hangzou, China, a public cycling scheme has been created with over 80,000 bikes and several thousand service points available for people to travel around the city without using cars. This scheme has contributed towards reducing the volume of traffic.

Management of essential resources, such as water, is also necessary for sustainable urban living; a city without water security is not sustainable. An example of a city which is managing its water resources to be sustainable is Singapore. The city has used a variety of methods including desalination, catching and storing rainwater, and recycling treated waste water to make the city's water supply secure without compromising the water resources of future generations.

Page 59 Classifying development - economic measures

1. A High Income Country (HIC) was defined by the World Bank in 2013 as a country with a GNI per capita of $12,476 or more.

2. Figure 1 shows that the majority of HICs are concentrated in the continents of Europe, North America and Oceania. The USA, Canada, Australia, New Zealand and all western and northern European countries are HICs. There are far fewer high income countries in Africa.

Page 60 Classifying development - social measures

One limitation of using a social measure of development is that the data provided could be inaccurate or unavailable. The data required for social measure indicators is often difficult to collect.

Page 61 The Demographic Transition Model

Birth rates are high in stage 1 of the DTM as populations at stage 1 tend to favour larger families, because having more children means there are more people earning an income. Societies in stage 1 of the DTM also have limited access to birth control, for example tribes living in the Amazon rainforest, which contributes to the high birth rate. A reason that death rates are high in stage 1 of the DTM is because of high infant mortality rates caused by limited access to medical care. Another reason for high death rates is low life expectancy, which could be caused by inadequate sanitation, disease or famine.

Page 62 Uneven development: causes and consequences

Uneven development is development that occurs at different rates in different areas. It can lead to international migration due to both push and pull factors. An example of a pull factor is the perceived opportunity of a better quality of life in another, more developed country. For example, people will often migrate to other countries in search of employment that provides a higher income than they could earn in their country of origin. An example of a push factor caused by uneven development is low life expectancy, which is more common in a less developed country, due to factors such as a lack of medical provision and adequate infrastructure to supply clean water. These factors may encourage people to migrate to a more developed country with a longer life expectancy and better healthcare.

Page 63 Reducing the global development gap

Intermediate technology is easy to use and maintain and doesn't require expensive foreign investment, so it enables people in low income countries to work self-sufficiently.

Page 64 Emerging India: changes

The secondary sector in India's economy has rapidly expanded in recent years. This has been encouraged by government initiatives such as Make in India, which is intended to make India a global manufacturing hub and create millions of jobs.

Page 65 Emerging India: impacts

There is more than one possible answer to this question. You could achieve maximum marks for agreeing or disagreeing with the statement provided you justify your answer with relevant reasons. Make sure you provide evidence to support your opinion and include a conclusion. Go to page 88 to see a model answer to this question.

Page 66 Causes of economic change

One way government policy has affected the decline in the primary and secondary sectors of the UK economy was the government's decision to sell off many nationalised industries, such as coal mining. This reduced the number of UK jobs available in these industries, which contributed to a decline in the primary and secondary sectors of the UK economy.

Page 67 Impacts of industry

One impact of industry on the UK's physical environment is contaminating the environment with industrial waste, which can cause soil pollution that destroys wildlife habitats.

Page 68 Rural landscape changes

One of the economic effects of population growth in rural landscapes is the impact upon the provision of key services; for example, in Northumberland the rise in migrants is creating increased levels of competition for jobs, resulting in a higher than average unemployment rate. A social effect of population growth in the rural areas of Northumberland is increased travelling times and traffic congestion caused by a higher number of commuters.

Page 69 Infrastructure improvements

Benefits of improvements to UK rail networks include reduced average journey times and providing enough services for the increasing numbers of people using train services. Projects like the HS2 (High Speed 2) also have the potential to improve connectivity between different areas of the UK and boost economic growth.

Page 70 The north–south divide

The north–south divide is an imaginary line that represents the differences between the quality of life of people in the north and south of the UK, with people in the south generally having a better quality of life than those in the north.

Page 71 The UK in the wider world

The installation of superfast broadband in the UK is improving the connectivity of the UK to the wider world, which is increasing online spending and investment from companies overseas, and helping to improve economic growth. It has also increased the UK's connectivity to the wider world by allowing UK businesses to communicate more easily with other countries.

Page 72 Types of resources

The countries with a usage of more than 500 million tonnes of oil equivalent are mainly located in the northern hemisphere, and include Russia and the USA. There are also some countries with this rate of energy consumption in the Middle East and Asia, such as India, whereas there are no countries with an energy consumption of 500 Mtoe or higher in Africa or Oceania.

Page 73 Food resources in the UK

(a) The value of the UK's imports of tea, coffee and cocoa was nearly £3 billion, whereas the value of UK exports of these products was only around £1.2 billion. Reasons for this may include the fact that tea, coffee and cocoa are all plant products, and therefore can only be grown in certain conditions. The UK is not suitable for growing them. These plants prefer a much warmer climate, so the UK has to import these products. Other reasons for the very high value of these imports are the expanding UK population, and the rise of a 'coffee shop culture' which has contributed to a greater demand for coffee and tea.

(b) Approximately £1.3 billion

Page 74 Water resources in the UK

The areas of serious water stress are in the south east and east of the UK. Areas of moderate water stress include parts of the south west, the West Midlands and parts of North Wales.

Page 75 Energy resources in the UK

Figure 1 shows that the consumption of oil (petroleum) in the UK, compared to other sources of energy, decreased after 1970 from approximately 43 per cent in 1970 to roughly 35 per cent in 1980. Since 1980, there has been relatively little change in UK oil consumption in comparison to other sources of energy.

Page 76 Distribution of food

Global food insecurity could be reduced by a more even distribution of existing food resources around the world. Currently, whilst many countries are experiencing food insecurity, others, especially more developed countries, such as the UK and the USA, have a surplus of food and a very high average calorie intake that is leading to major obesity problems. If this surplus of food was supplied to countries where people do not have enough food instead, it would help to reduce food insecurity. Global food insecurity could also be reduced by addressing the factors which can have an impact on food supply, such as pests and diseases. The impact of these factors could be reduced by making pesticides and herbicides more affordable for farmers in low income countries, which would help prevent reduced crop yields, and by making better use of advanced technology, such as the use of aeroponics and hydroponics, to grow food crops in different places. This could lead to a higher rate of global food production, which would help to reduce global food insecurity.

Page 77 Impacts of food insecurity

Any two of the following impacts: rising food prices, because a reduced supply of staple crops, such as rice and wheat, can increase the prices suppliers are able to charge; social unrest; soil erosion caused by overgrazing, deforestation and overcultivation; undernutrition, when people lack a reliable supply of sufficient nutritious food over a long period of time; reduced capacity to work; or famine.

Page 78 Increasing food supply

One of the advantages of the Indus Basin Irrigation System in Pakistan is that farmers have improved access to water supplies, which means that crop yields have improved, providing a more plentiful supply of food and higher incomes. The agricultural products of the area now constitute 23 per cent of Pakistan's GDP. An advantage of the creation of the Mangla and Tarbela reservoirs as part of the development is that fishing in them provides an additional source of protein, which has improved the diet of local people.

Page 79 Sustainable food options

1. One way food supplies can be made more sustainable is organic farming, which uses natural techniques instead of chemicals. It is more sustainable because it is better for the soil and better for ecosystems around agricultural land – for example, it doesn't use chemicals which harm bees and other pollinating insects. The sustainability of food supplies can also be increased through more people eating seasonally, which involves eating food which is locally sourced when it is naturally at its best. This increases sustainability because it reduces food miles, and therefore global carbon emissions, and it also supports the livelihoods of small local producers, which will help to ensure their farms are successful businesses. Finally, reducing waste is arguably one of the most important ways of increasing the sustainability of food supplies. Growing, harvesting, packaging, storing and transporting food requires large amounts of resources, so throwing away large volumes of edible food, as the UK currently does, is completely unsustainable. Reducing waste would increase efficiency and sustainability by increasing the number of people that could be fed with the existing levels of food produced. *You could also have mentioned: urban farming initiatives; permaculture; sustainably sourced fish and meat.*

2. An advantage of the Rwanda Aid project is that farmers are able to create a stable income from their produce. A disadvantage is that to date, training isn't available for everyone.

Page 80 Distribution of water

One of the reasons for the increase in global water consumption is the growth in the world's population, which is increasing by 80 million people per year, leading to rising demands for water supplies for domestic and agricultural needs. Also, increased affluence has resulted in lifestyle and diet changes in NEEs. More people are now eating diets with larger quantities of dairy and meat products, which require large volumes of water to produce. *You could also have mentioned biofuels.*

Page 81 Impacts of water insecurity

The demand for water supplies can lead to conflict in some places around the world as governments and people compete for enough supplies to meet their own demands. Conflict is particularly likely in places where water resources cross international borders. For example, dams in Turkey affect the water supply of countries downstream such as Syria and Iraq. If Turkey's water use resulted in severe water shortages in these countries, it could cause civil unrest or even war.

Page 82 Increasing water supply

The South–North Water Diversion Project in China is a large-scale water transfer project which is designed to transfer water from the south of China to the drier north-east. An advantage of the scheme is that it improves water supplies for agriculture in the north, which should lead to increased crop yields and income for farmers. A major disadvantage of the project was that it resulted in the relocation of 330,000 people, causing major disruption to their lives.

Page 83 Sustainable water options

Local schemes organised by NGOs like WaterAid are vital for providing people in LICs and NEEs with a reliable supply of clean water, because often the governments of these countries cannot afford to invest in the infrastructure to provide everybody with clean water. Local schemes to improve water supplies mean that people, often women and children, don't have to spend hours collecting water, so they are able to attend school instead. Also, having access to supplies of clean water reduces the risk of waterborne diseases like cholera caused by drinking polluted water. This means the quality of life for many poorer villagers is significantly improved.

Page 84 Distribution of energy

One of the factors that affects energy supply is whether physical conditions are suitable for generating energy. For example, Iceland has an abundance of geothermal energy because it is located in a tectonically active area. A second factor is the ability to develop technology to harness new energy resources, such as fracking to extract shale gas. Politics are also a factor affecting energy supply, as unrest or war can prevent the efficient extraction and export of fossil fuels such as oil. *You could also have mentioned the cost of exploitation and production and whether climatic conditions are suitable for generating solar power.*

Page 85 Impacts of energy insecurity

With rising demands for energy, countries are becoming more reliant on importing supplies, increasing their dependency on other countries. Unrest in areas like the Middle East creates uncertainties, leading to increases in oil prices, which can also cause local unrest and conflict. Many modern day wars are, in part, caused by the desire to control valuable oil and natural gas assets.

Page 86 Increasing energy supply

Oil extraction from the Athabasca tar sands in Canada has several advantages and disadvantages. An advantage of extracting the oil is that it has provided a secure source of energy, meaning Canada is not reliant on importing energy resources for its people. A disadvantage is the environmental impacts of fuel extraction. This has included the removal of forest, which damaged wildlife habitats, and pollution of the Athabasca River from leaking pipes. *There are other examples you could have mentioned on the page.*

Page 87 Sustainable energy options

1. Strategies for sustainable energy use can be implemented on different scales. Individuals can use energy more sustainably in the home by using energy-efficient lightbulbs, installing double-glazing, and installing cavity wall and loft insulation. These measures reduce the amount of heat escaping, leading to less energy used to keep homes warm. Hotels can use energy more sustainably by adopting a 'no wash' policy for towels unless specifically asked by guests. This means they use less energy to do washing. Transport can also be made more sustainable, for example, creating bike sharing schemes such as those used in Copenhagen, Denmark, and by investment in public transport systems, such as rail networks in order to encourage people to use their cars less.

2. The Belo Monte Dam in Brazil has created job opportunities. However, it has also disrupted about 12,000 local people.

Page 88 Making geographical decisions

There is more than one possible answer to this question. You could achieve maximum marks for agreeing or disagreeing with the statement provided you justify your answer with relevant reasons. Make sure you provide evidence to support your opinion and include a conclusion. Use information from pages 14 and 15 to help you with your answer.

Page 89 Issue evaluation

Variations in wealth can affect access to key infrastructure, such as piped water, which in turn can result in differences in water quality.

Page 90 Written sources

C 6 in 10 people worldwide lack safely managed sanitation

Page 91 Issue evaluation

Project 2 has the potential to significantly improve the quality of life and socio-economic conditions for the rural poor in Ghana, as the project will, in time, improve both water supply and sanitation services in rural areas. Access to a secure supply of safe, clean water is key to improving socio-economic conditions, although as **Figure 1** reports, 2.1 billion people do not have access to safe, readily available water at home. Without this, people in rural areas can spend hours a day travelling to collect water, which may be contaminated, leaving them vulnerable to waterborne diseases that limit life expectancy. Safe, available water is also essential for economic development, as it is necessary for agriculture and industrial production, and if people are often ill due to poor sanitation and contaminated water, they cannot go to school or work, limiting productivity and long-term development.

Project 2 will improve both water and sanitation services. The access to water is likely to have an immediate positive impact upon social conditions for women and children, as they are the members of the community who would have had to travel long distances to collect water previously (as shown in the photograph in **Figure 1**, and described in **Figure 4**). Women like Zuwera, named in **Figure 4**, will be able to send their children to school in the future, rather than send them to fetch water. This will have a positive long-term socio-economic impact, as children will be able to get a better education, improving their employment prospects in later life.

Similarly, Project 2 is funded by the World Bank, so it is likely to have a large enough budget to install permanent infrastructure which will greatly improve sanitation facilities, such as flushing toilets and sewerage pipes. In contrast, Project 1 seems to be a smaller scale scheme which will have a smaller budget. These sanitation facilities are likely to improve basic hygiene in rural areas; currently, as **Figure 1** reports, 892 million people defecate in the open, which contributes to the spread of bacteria and therefore disease, and it is a growing problem in sub-Saharan African countries such as Ghana. Proper toilets in rural areas would prevent this, and help to reduce the population's vulnerability to disease. This will greatly improve quality of life, as decreased levels of disease will improve life expectancy, and it will also improve economic conditions, as if people are healthy they will be able to work more and earn money.

One aspect of Project 2 which may not be advantageous to improving quality of life for the rural poor in Ghana is that the scope of the project is nationwide, and it will begin in urban areas, probably because urban centres are likely to generate a larger percentage of the country's GDP. Prioritising urban areas means that it may take much longer for the project to improve conditions for Ghana's rural poor than a smaller scale project like Project 1 would. However, this drawback is offset by the projected size of Project 2; as it is a large-scale project which is targeted towards the whole country, it will eventually improve quality of life and socio-economic conditions for many more people than a smaller project will.

In conclusion, Project 2 would effectively improve the quality of life and socio-economic conditions for the rural poor in Ghana, because its improvement of sanitation services is likely to significantly reduce vulnerability to disease, which will directly improve health and therefore quality of life and life expectancy. This in turn is likely to increase economic conditions, as more people will be able to go to school and work, and therefore gain an education and improve their economic prospects.

Page 92 Making enquiries
Risk = misjudging the tide, leading to potential danger of drowning.
Reduce the risk = checking the times of high and low tide before commencing fieldwork.

Page 93 Measuring and recording data
When explaining about your own fieldwork, you will need to provide clear evidence that you are writing about your own investigation. For example, when writing about your data collection methods, be specific about how you conducted the techniques. For example, to collect qualitative data about opinions on quality of life in two urban areas, we used a stratified sampling method to obtain information from different age groups when we conducted our questionnaire.

Page 94 Processing and presenting data
When talking about the advantages and disadvantages of your chosen data presentation techniques, remember to be specific about their effectiveness in presenting the data.
For example, to display data on the profile of the river at the three sites, we used a line graph. An advantage of a line graph is that it enables comparisons between the profiles to be analysed accurately.

Page 95 Analysis, conclusions and evaluations
To achieve the higher marks in this question your answer should include several clear explanations that develop specific fieldwork points; ongoing evaluation that continually refers to the reliability of the results collected and a balanced conclusion.

Page 96 Map skills
The majority of earthquakes occur along plate boundaries, particularly along the west side of the South American plate, forming a linear pattern of earthquakes along the west side of South and Central America, and around the edge of the Pacific plate. There are far fewer earthquakes which are not located at plate boundaries, and these are much more dispersed, for example the earthquakes located in the middle of the Eurasian plate.

Page 97 Grid references and scale
(a) 5724

(b) 568247

(c) 1.5 km

Page 98 Cross sections and contours
Approximately 203 metres above sea level

Page 99 Interpreting map features
Wilton has a nucleated settlement pattern, as the buildings are grouped closely together.

Page 100 Using photos
Possible answers include: Label = river cliff, meander, valley
Annotation = a river cliff is formed by erosional processes like hydraulic action, where the river erodes and undercuts the outside bank.

Page 101 Graphs
1. A bar chart
2. Positive correlation
3. A line chart or a histogram

Page 102 Maps and pyramids
3.3 million

Page 103 Statistical skills
13 per cent

Published by BBC Active, an imprint of Educational Publishers LLP, part of the Pearson Education Group, 80 Strand, London, WC2R 0RL.
www.pearsonschools.co.uk/BBCBitesize

© Educational Publishers LLP 2018
BBC logo © BBC 1996. BBC and BBC Active are trademarks of the British Broadcasting Corporation.

Typeset by Jouve India Private Limited
Produced and illustrated by Elektra Media Ltd
Cover design by Andrew Magee & Pearson Education Limited 2018
Cover illustration by Darren Lingard / Oxford Designers & Illustrators

The right of Michael Chiles to be identified as author of this work has been asserted by him in accordance with the Copyright, Designs and Patents Act 1988.

First published 2018

21 20 19 18
10 9 8 7 6 5 4 3 2 1

British Library Cataloguing in Publication Data
A catalogue record for this book is available from the British Library
ISBN 978 1 406 68601 2

Note from the publisher
Pearson has robust editorial processes, including answer and fact checks, to ensure the accuracy of the content in this publication, and every effort is made to ensure this publication is free of errors. We are, however, only human, and occasionally errors do occur. Pearson is not liable for any misunderstandings that arise as a result of errors in this publication, but it is our priority to ensure that the content is accurate. If you spot an error, please do contact us at resourcescorrections@pearson.com so we can make sure it is corrected.

Acknowledgements
The authors and publisher would like to thank the following individuals and organisations for their kind permission to reproduce copyright material.
Page 97, 99: © Crown copyright 2017, OS 100030901.
Page 98: © Crown copyright 2017, OS 100030901.
Page 90: Reprinted from "2.1 billion people lack safe drinking water at home, more than twice as many lack safe sanitation", Copyright (2017)", http://www.who.int/mediacentre/news/releases/2017/water-sanitation-hygiene/en/

Photographs
(Key: b-bottom; c-centre; l-left; r-right; t-top)
123RF: Kavram 006l; **Alamy Stock Photo**: Banana Pancake iiit, 051t, David Gowans iiib, 051b, Peter Eastland 006r, Imagegallery2 011, Neil Cooper 012, Robert Timoney 013, Steven May 014, Steffen Binke 017, Design Pics Inc 023, Wildlife GmbH 026, Mr. Nut 033, Alan Curtis 034, Terry Whittaker 035, Eyesite 039, Midland Aerial Pictures 040, Paul Boyes 041, james jagger 043br, Ashley Hugo 043t, David Wrench/LGPL 048l, Drew Buckley 048r, PearlBucknall 050, Anne Marie Palmer 054, Jeff Morgan 07 067, Greg Balfour Evans 069l, Jeff Gilbert 069r, Ron Nickel/Design Pics Inc 083, Rolf Hicker/mauritius images GmbH 085, Ashley Cooper 086, Ian Dagnall Commercial Collection 092, RosaIreneBetancourt12 093r, Martin Shields 093l, Carl Johnson/Design Pics Inc 100b; **Nasa:** Goddard Space Flight Center 100t; **Reuters Images**: Gennady Galperin 028, Stian Bergel 087; **Rex Features**: Mark Pearson 045; **Shutterstock**: Halel2uya vi, Dainis Derics 016, Dubassy 031, Stonja 043bl, Zhukova Valentyna 058, HYPERLINK "https://premier.shutterstock.com/image/contributor/545479" Alison Hancock 079, Zeljko Radojko 082, Martchan 090
All other images © Pearson Education

Websites
Pearson Education Limited is not responsible for the content of third-party websites.